W9-ACE-828

Secrets of

TAROT

Secrets of

TAROT

ANNIE LIONNET

A Dorling Kindersley Book

Dorling **DK** Kindersley

LONDON, NEW YORK, SYDNEY, DELHI, PARIS,
MUNICH, and JOHANNESBURG

First published in the United States of America in 2000 by
Dorling Kindersley Publishing Inc.
Madison Avenue, New York, New York, 10016

This book was conceived, designed, and produced by
THE IVY PRESS LIMITED,
The Old Candlemakers, Lewes, East Sussex BN7 2NZ

Art director *Peter Bridgewater*
Editorial director *Sophie Collins*
Designers *Kevin Knight, Jane Lanaway, Alistair Plumb*
Editors *Rowan Davies and April McCroskie*
Picture researchers *Vanessa Fletcher*
Photography *Guy Ryecart*
Photography organization *Kay MacMullan*
Illustrations *Sarah Young, Lesley Ann Hutchings*

A CIP catalog record for this book is
available from the Library of Congress

ISBN 0 7894 6780 1

Originated and printed by
Hong Kong Graphic and Printing Limited, China

see our complete
catalog at
www.dk.com

CONTENTS

Variety
There are many Tarot designs from which to choose.

HOW TO USE THIS BOOK

To make *Secrets of Tarot* easy to use it has been split into three sections. The first section gives all the background information you need about the history and development of the Tarot. The second section explains each card and its meaning within the Tarot. In the final section, this book shows you how to put what you have learned to practical use, utilizing case studies as examples for you to follow.

Important Notice

Even today the Tarot is sometimes regarded with suspicion. There is absolutely nothing to fear from the Tarot as the cards are simply an ancient method of divination allowing us to understand the spiritual patterns and aspirations that run through our lives. However, it is very important to foster an attitude of respect for the cards and the sacred images on them. This will ensure a safe, happy, and rewarding relationship with the Tarot.

Practical information
Practical pages like these tell you about the different elements of Tarot reading.

Card guides
These pages are a comprehensive guide to each group of cards.

Detail
Detailed pages supplement the guides, telling you about each card in detail.

Application
These pages show the practicalities of Tarot readings, using case studies as examples.

The Mysteries of the Tarot

Watercarrier
*The Watercarrier pours water
from two jugs, blending the
different aspects of life.*

The Tarot belongs to the Western Mystery Tradition and is one of the most enigmatic systems of prediction and divination. Even the origins of the Tarot remain shrouded in mystery. Similarly, it is not known exactly how the Tarot works or how it is able to provide us with a mirror image of our current situation. This has continued to fascinate all who have consulted the Tarot over the hundreds of years that it has been in existence.

Some people believe in the presence of a higher intelligence that in some way directs the shuffling and selection of the cards, so that the appropriate cards appear in the right order. Others believe that Carl Jung's theory of synchronicity is in operation when we consult the cards. He suggested that everything in the universe is connected, and our outer world is a mirror of our inner world. As there is no separate reality, the question asked will be reflected in the selection of the card. Even if this theory appears to be somewhat far-fetched and the choice of cards is arbitrary, each card seems to contain symbolism and the power to interpret events accurately.

Divination and symbolism

All over the world, symbolic languages have been developed to access the secrets of the human psyche. This is called divination, from the Latin *divinare* meaning "to divine." When we consult the cards, we are doing a divination and seeking to understand the spiritual patterns, aspirations, and hidden motivations that underlie our lives. The symbols and images that the Tarot pictures illustrate create a bridge between the conscious and unconscious, and connect us with our strengths and weaknesses, our potential, and the aspects of our nature that can sometimes undermine us or prevent us from developing that potential.

The mystic symbolism of the Tarot describes our journey through life and encompasses all the archetypal experiences that we are likely to have. These coded symbols contain the secrets of the human heart and, according to some, the divine law of the universe. Understanding the mysteries of the Tarot is to understand the mystery of our own lives and the blueprint that we all carry within us.

The Inner Self

Tarot cards can be used to tap into our inner psyche and discover more about ourselves by addressing all the different facets of our nature.

TAROT DEFINED

The Tarot is a book of knowledge and wisdom portrayed in pictures and symbols. When you choose a card, it will reflect an inner image of yourself or an outer experience, as well as revealing the meaning of that particular situation. Sometimes this will confirm what you already know about yourself, but the truth you are being shown can sometimes come as a surprise. We all possess a natural intuitive ability that we do not always fully trust. Working with the symbols and images of the Tarot can help develop that innate skill so that we can be more in tune with our deeper selves and use our intuition in our everyday lives.

Origins and History of the Tarot

Italian origins

It is generally thought that the roots of modern-day Tarot lie in Renaissance Italy.

The origins of the Tarot are lost in the mists of time and there has been much speculation about when it was first used. Some say that its roots lie in Egypt, China, India, or Persia, but the truth remains elusive. One theory suggests that it was brought to Europe by gypsies, but what we can be more sure of is that the Tarot as we know it today dates back to the Renaissance. In the 15th century an aristocratic Italian family commissioned several Tarot packs to be painted. These historic packs are now housed in museums and private collections, but one of them, which remains virtually intact, contains the standard 78 cards that are used today as the basis of the modern Tarot deck.

Origins of the Tarot design

Many of the early packs are French in design, the Tarot de Marseilles being a well-known example. In the 17th century the Italians stopped manufacturing cards and they began to be imported from France. The 78-card deck has been used in many different ways over the hundreds of years that it has been in existence, although it is more than likely that it was originally used as a card game called *tarot* in France and *tarocco* in Italy.

Associations with the Devil

During the Middle Ages the Church burned many sets of Tarot cards because it was vehemently opposed to the pagan imagery on the cards. Even today the Tarot is sometimes referred to as "the Devil's picturebook" and looked upon with fear and suspicion. Some of the very early packs replaced the Pope and Papess cards with the High Priest and the High Priestess to avoid Roman Catholic associations.

In spite of religious opposition, card games, whether for fun, gambling, or divination, continued to flourish. By the end of the 18th century, however, the esoteric and divinatory meaning of the cards was in evidence, and this is what most people associate them with today.

Tarot de Marseilles

This classic deck from the 16th century was hugely influential on card designs. Throughout this book we have presented a variety of Tarot decks.

WHAT'S IN A TAROT PACK?

The Tarot is made up of 78 cards and is divided into the Major Arcana and the Minor Arcana, from the Latin word *arcanum* meaning "mystery" or "secret."

 THE MAGICIAN

 THE HIGH PRIESTESS

 THE EMPRESS

 THE EMPEROR

 THE HIEROPHANT

 THE LOVERS

 THE CHARIOT

 STRENGTH

 THE HERMIT

 WHEEL OF FORTUNE

 JUSTICE

 THE HANGED MAN

 DEATH

 TEMPERANCE

 THE DEVIL

 THE TOWER

 THE STAR

 THE MOON

 THE SUN

 JUDGEMENT

 THE WORLD

 THE FOOL

The Major Arcana
The 22 cards depict different stages of human development.

The Minor Arcana
The 56 cards expand themes from the Major Arcana and indicate possible future events.

| THE WANDS | THE SWORDS | THE PENTACLES | THE CUPS |

15

Tarot Symbolism: The Major and Minor Arcana

Major Arcana
This is one of the 22 cards of the Major Arcana, which reflect important events in our lives.

four court cards: the Page, the Knight, the Queen, and the King. The Minor Arcana cards offer very specific information about our circumstances and experiences and identify in which direction the Querent (the person having their cards read) may be heading. The meaning of each Minor Arcana card incorporates the meaning associated with the element of each suit and the number of the pip cards. The gender of the court cards is also taken into consideration.

Complementary principles

Throughout history many spiritual disciplines have spoken about two opposite but complementary principles at work in the universe. The Chinese call these *yin* and *yang*, the feminine and masculine principle. When a person is psychologically well-balanced and "whole," he or she has integrated both feminine and masculine traits. Many of the Major Arcana cards

The Major Arcana consists of 22 cards numbered 1–21 and the unnumbered Fool card. These are the trump cards of the Tarot, and their powerful symbolism reflects the major events in our lives. The Minor Arcana consists of 56 cards made up of four suits: Cups, Wands, Pentacles, and Swords. Each suit has 14 cards from ace to ten, known as pip cards, plus

represent aspects of either the feminine or masculine principle, while in the Minor Arcana, the suits of Wands and Swords are masculine, and the Cups and Pentacles are feminine.

Symbolic themes

Three of the most important symbolic themes in the Tarot are gender, numbers, and elements. Numbers are also associated with masculine and feminine principles. The meaning of each Minor Arcana card is based to a large extent on its number, as well as the suit to which it belongs. The significance of the numbered Major Arcana cards is less, since each card can be identified without a number. Fire and air are associated with masculine traits, and water and earth with feminine.

The Four Suits

The four suits of the Minor Arcana can be learned about in more detail by referring to pages 84–141.

Style-conscious
It is best to choose your deck according to the design and style that most appeals to you.

CHOOSING A TAROT DECK
There is a wealth of Tarot packs from which to choose, each with its own history and design. Even though each pack has evolved in its own unique way and the pictorial images of the cards can differ considerably, the essence of what each card is saying remains the same. It is important to choose a pack that stimulates your imagination and has a visual style that you really like.

French
The Lovers from the Tarot de Marseilles.

Egyptian
The Lovers from the Egipcios Kier Tarot.

Spiritual
The Lovers from the Tarot of the Spirit.

Historical
The Lovers from the
Visconti Sforza Tarot.

Artistic
The Lovers from the
Morgan-Greer Tarot.

Oriental
The Lovers from
the Ukiyoe Tarot.

Development of Tarot Design

The Torah
*Much Jewish
mysticism finds
its basis in
the Torah.*

The 78-card deck we use today is said to have originated in Italy, but it is the Marseilles deck designs that are accepted as standard. In the late 19th century three members of the Societas Rosicruciana formed the Hermetic Order of the Golden Dawn, and this marked a turning point in the development of the Tarot.

Influence of the Golden Dawn

Members of the Hermetic Order of the Golden Dawn developed the correlation between the cabbala, the mystical element of Judaism, the cabbalist belief in the 22 paths of the Tree of Life, and the Tarot. One of the founders, Samuel McGregor Mathers, changed the numerical sequence of the Major Arcana and put the Fool before card number 1 rather than after card number 21, as well as switching around the Strength and Justice cards. The Order also incorporated astrology into its interpretations and greatly extended the correlation between the Tarot and the astrological elements, planets, and zodiac signs.

The Thoth deck

Aleister Crowley joined the Hermetic Order of the Golden Dawn in 1898, but after disagreements he left and in 1905 formed his own order, Argenteum Astrum. His teachings on the Tarot elaborated and extended those of the Golden Dawn and are extremely complex. He reinterpreted the symbolism of the Tarot and designed his own deck, known as the Thoth deck. He believed that the Fool should be the first card in the Major Arcana sequence and be numbered 0.

The Rider-Waite deck

In 1916 another member of the Golden Dawn, Arthur Edward Waite, had worked on the design of a new Tarot deck with the artist Pamela Colman Smith, and this became known as the Rider-Waite pack. At the time, its creators received a lot of criticism for the changes that they made and for lack of aesthetics. In spite of such hostility and resistance to this new pack, their interpretations made the Tarot more accessible and comprehensible than other more obscure designs, and today it is one of the most widely used packs.

Tree of Life

Like the Tarot, the Tree of Life has 10 emanations. The Tree of Life has 4 elements, and the Tarot has 4 suits to represent the elements. See page 109 for more information.

Wanderer
*The Fool from the
Papus Tarot.*

DECKS

Selecting a deck is a very individual choice. Some of the most popular and best-known Tarots in use today are the Rider-Waite pack, the Marseilles, and the J J Swiss packs. The latter dates back to the 19th century and got its name from using the Roman gods Jupiter and Juno instead of the Pope and Papess. Many unusual packs exist such as the Elemental Tarot, the Motherpeace Tarot, and the Mystic Tarot. All are based on a particular philosophy or mythology.

Carefree	**Colorful**	**Childlike**
The Fool from the Universal Waite Tarot.	*The Fool from the Oswald Wirth Tarot.*	*The Fool from the Golden Dawn Tarot.*

0 THE FOOL

Serious

The Fool from the Witches Tarot.

The Fool

Ethereal

The Fool from the Haindl Tarot.

Acrobatic

The Fool from the Motherpeace Tarot.

How to Choose Your Tarot Deck

There are several points to consider when choosing a deck. Assuming that you buy your own pack, it is important that it appeals to you visually and speaks to you in some way. Ideally you should be able to view a sample deck so that you are able to see all of the cards. You may feel drawn to one or two images, or like the feel of the whole deck. Some people like to familiarize themselves with one pack and work exclusively with the one they know the best, while others will interact with more than one pack and use them for different purposes.

Arthur Waite
Arthur Edward Waite's deck, designed with Pamela Colman Smith, was a best-seller.

Good vibrations

The type of pack that you choose will depend a lot on your interests and background, as well as what you feel intuitively attracted to. There is certainly no shortage of decks to choose from. People often find that working with the images and symbols of the Tarot begins to heighten their intuitive powers. It is important to use your own deck and not one that belongs, or has belonged, to someone else. This is because you need to form a relationship with the cards that is personal to you, and this is not possible if somebody else has already imprinted their own psychic vibration on the cards. You do not have to buy your own deck; someone may buy you a set that you happen to like.

Famous decks

In 1909 Arthur Edward Waite teamed up with Pamela Colman Smith and devised a set of cards published by the Rider Company. While Waite made changes to the Major Arcana, Smith concentrated on the artwork of the Minor Arcana. For the first time every card had a scene on it and this meant that the Minor Arcana was open to more interpretation. This was unique at the time and the Rider-Waite pack became a best-seller.

Aleister Crowley's mysterious deck was illustrated for him by Lady Frieda Harris. He earned a negative reputation for some of his bizarre magical practices and became a notorious devotee of the occult. His teachings on the Tarot went beyond those of the Order of the Golden Dawn (see p20). The pair's ideas were first published in 1944 as *The Book of Thoth*; the actual cards were finally published, posthumously for both, in 1969.

Fiery
*The Tower from the
Golden Dawn Tarot.*

SELECTING A DECK
Choose the pack for yourself.
It will help you develop your own intuitive and perhaps psychic abilities and,
as a result, give much better readings. The Mythic Tarot will appeal to those
interested in Greek mythology, while the Celtic or Arthurian packs will hold a
special fascination for those who resonate with Celtic mythology. If neither of
these areas is of particular interest to you, the more universal appeal of the
Rider-Waite pack might be a good starting place.

African
*The Tower from the Royal
Fez Moroccan Tarot.*

Powerful
*The Tower from
the Papus Tarot.*

Dramatic
*The Tower from the
Astrological Tarot.*

Gazing
*The Tower from
the Gypsy Tarot.*

THE TOWER
LA MAISON DIEU

Eye-opener
*The Tower from
the Thoth Tarot.*

XVI

The Tower

Horticultural
*The Tower from
the Herbal Tarot.*

XVI The Tower

Tarot Ritual

The reading
It is important to create
the right atmosphere for
a Tarot reading.

Whatever your approach to the Tarot, it is important that you cultivate an attitude of respect for the sacred images portrayed on the cards. This will become more apparent as you connect with them on a deeper level. Once you have selected a Tarot pack, it is a good idea to spend time examining the cards one by one. In this way, you start to form a relationship with them and, rather like osmosis, slowly begin to absorb their symbolism and imagery. The next step is to start reading and learning the

divinatory meaning of each card. Do not expect to grasp the whole meaning of every card right away—it will take time to understand their complexity.

Establishing the atmosphere
Creating the right frame of mind before you begin working with the Tarot is most important. Ideally, you need to create a quiet and still atmosphere when beginning to look at the cards, as well as before a reading. Some of the ways you can do this are by taking the phone off the hook, lighting some incense and a candle, playing some soft music, saying a prayer, or perhaps doing a ritual invocation with which you feel comfortable. If you prefer, you could say a prayer such as this one used by the Golden Dawn: *In the divine name IAO, invoke thee from Great Angel HRU who art set over the operations of this secret wisdom. Lay thine hand invisibly on these consecrated cards of art, that I may obtain knowledge of hidden things, to the glory of the ineffable name, Amen.* You could place

each card on a black silk cloth and meditate on the picture to see what impressions you receive. Alternatively, think about the meaning of each card and how that card speaks to you.

Card meanings

There is much debate about the validity of reversed cards: the idea of giving different interpretations to upright and reversed cards is fairly recent. Some people assign a different meaning to a reversed card and find it easier to interpret because the meaning of the card becomes less ambiguous. Although this simplifies the divination, it does deny something that is implicit in understanding astrology and many other esoteric disciplines. These ancient systems believe that everything contains positive and negative aspects, and that inherent in everything is its opposite.

Consultations

For further information on setting the right atmosphere for a reading, see page 144; 'Preparing to Consult the Cards.'

LAPIS LAZULI

Crystals
These are used for the cleansing and psychic protection of the cards.

BLOODSTONE

ENERGIZING THE CARDS
As you handle the cards and interact with them you will begin to energize the pack. You can also do this in a more focused way by creating a circle and laying the cards on your black silk cloth within the circle. Some people like to place crystals in certain positions, say, at each corner of the table. Each crystal has its own property but some of the best ones to use are amethyst, lapis lazuli, tiger's eye, topaz, and turquoise. Use your own intuition to decide which ones you most like to work with.

Ritual
Salt, scented water, incense, and candles are ideal ways to prepare your space for a reading.

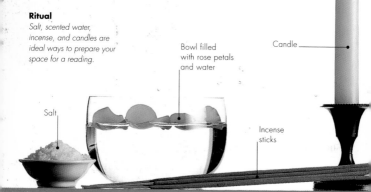

Candle

Bowl filled
with rose petals
and water

Salt

Incense
sticks

Bloodstone
This crystal is
considered to aid
clairvoyance.

Lapis Lazuli
This crystal is thought
to transmit psychic
influences.

Agate
These layered crystals
are believed to quell
anxiety.

Tiger's Eye
This crystal is thought
to signify success and
strong willpower.

Silk
*Wrapping the cards
in black silk protects
them from psychic
contamination.*

Boxed set
*Placing the silk-wrapped cards
in a beautiful wooden box
preserves their sacred quality
and importance.*

Protect
your cards

Special
container

Personalizing
Your Tarot Rituals

Your space
*Create a sacred space in
a way that feels personal
and comfortable for you.*

S alt has long been used in
cleansing and psychic protection
rituals and you can apply this by
passing a dish of saltwater over the
laid-out cards. You can then follow that
with a lighted incense stick of pine or
rosemary and hold a golden, yellow,
or red candle above the cards. Finally,
pass a dish of rose petals in water or
an essential oil of rose or lavender over
the cards. Leave the cards in the circle
for 24 hours before putting them away.

You can then wrap them in the black
silk cloth and put them in a beautiful
wooden box or some other container
that feels special to you. The idea
behind wrapping the cards like this
is that black is a neutral color and
prevents the cards from absorbing
outside vibrations. Using silk is a further
way of marking them sacred to you and
preventing them from being psychically
contaminated. Keeping them in a
special cloth or box symbolizes the
respect and value that the cards hold.

The importance of simplicity

Remember that you do not have to
follow this ritual unless it feels right for
you. Find your own way of creating a
sacred space and preparing yourself
for a reading. The important thing to
remember if you are using some form of
ritual when working with the Tarot is not
to create too great a dependency on
the ritual itself. Use it as a simple way
of becoming attuned and creating the

right mind-set. If you firmly believe in some kind of ceremony before doing a reading, it is important that you should observe that. On the other hand, if you have a more relaxed attitude, you shouldn't feel pressurized into adopting a ritualistic approach. Finding your own way is what matters."

Guidance offered by the Tarot

When you ask a question, the Tarot will reflect everything that revolves around that situation, as well as showing the path that you are most likely to follow. It can identify what will help and hinder you along the way and the optimum way in which to proceed. The choice is always yours as to whether or not you follow the guidance offered.

Psychic Powers

Tarot reading will not suddenly give you psychic powers, but if you are lucky enough to have psychic tendencies then the Tarot may enhance them.

THE CARDS
AND THEIR MEANING

The Tarot cards represent the symbolic journey of the Querent through life. The Tarot cannot predict a fixed and fated future, rather it describes the quality and meaning of a given moment in an individual's life. Often the reading will describe past events in the context of the present and bring to light choices and motives, as well as their cause and effect. We can be unaware of the underlying reasons for our behavior, and the cards can offer a deeper awareness of what goes on beneath the surface. These insights have the potential to offer us greater freedom and choice in the future.

An Introduction to the Major and Minor Arcana

Justice

This card represents balance and is shown with the scales and sword of justice.

Human nature is complex, and because the Tarot represents a mirror of the soul, it reflects this complexity back to us.

Major Arcana

The beginning of the Querent's journey through life is specifically represented by the Fool. The other 21 cards describe aspects of the Querent himself and other personalities that he will meet, as well as situations he will encounter and the qualities he will need to cope with them.

When you are interpreting the meanings of the Major Arcana cards you will sometimes find them ambiguous and even contradictory. Each Tarot reader has his own unique interpretation, but one good rule of thumb is to decide which aspects of each card are most relevant in the context of the whole reading. You can then take into consideration how the cards work together rather than seeing them in isolation.

Aspects of any card can also reflect the Querent at the time of consulting the cards. The Major Arcana describes both our outer reality and the situations that come to meet us over which we often feel we have no control, as well as the deeper spiritual dimension that lies beneath the surface of our day-to-day lives. Often the appearance of a card comes as a surprise to the Querent, as he was not aware of that particular aspect of himself and how it affected both him and others.

Minor Arcana

The 56 cards of the Minor Arcana are divided into the four suits of Cups, Wands, Pentacles, and Swords. Each suit contains ten numbered cards—the pip cards—and four court cards. The court cards portray influential people in the Querent's life but can also reveal his own attributes, of which he may not be aware. The numbered cards represent the experiences and decisions that can illuminate the Querent's motives and suggest future directions he might take.

Shuffling

It is a good idea to shuffle the cards face down on a flat surface. This way the cards will get turned around and will offer up the possibility of reversed cards during a reading.

OPTIMISM AND GUIDANCE

The Querent sets out on her spiritual journey eagerly and with a light heart. Challenges might lie ahead but the Fool is unconcerned with the possibility of failure or trouble along the way. The Magician signifies guidance en route, possibly offering direction to capitalize on opportunities and to beware of traps and dangers that might lie ahead. Youthful optimism often needs to be tempered with some caution.

Oriental
*The Fool from
the Ukiyoe Tarot.*

Ragged
*The Fool from the
Visconti Sforza Tarot.*

Mysterious
*The Magician from
the Thoth Tarot.*

I

ל The Magician ☿

The MAGICIAN
1

Shamanistic
*The Magician from the
Shining Woman Tarot.*

Fool and Magician

The Fool

The Fool represents new beginnings, untapped potential, and a fresh start in life. Often some kind of risk is required and a willingness to jump into the unknown. The Querent is being urged to move forward and take on a new challenge. However, the outcome may be uncertain, so an act of faith is required on his part if he is to follow this course.

This card depicts an innocent-looking and carefree youth setting out on a journey, blissfully unaware of the fact that his next step could lead to his downfall. If this card appears in a spread, new opportunities could be on the horizon. However, not everything will go according to plan and we should expect the unexpected. The Querent is about to embark on a journey of self-discovery and could be in for some surprising revelations. Although this card suggests that the Querent will have the confidence and idealism to throw him into the next phase of life, it warns against blind faith

Magician
The Magician signifies guidance either inherent in the Querent, or from an outside source.

and not being foolishly naive when faced with certain choices. Some caution or circumspection is advised.

The Magician

The Magician has mastery and control of the four elements and the four suit symbols, which suggests that the Querent has the imagination, determination, self-confidence, and inherent gifts required to promote himself and to develop his current and latent abilities. When the Magician appears in a spread it is an indication that the Querent should look for opportunities to use his talents, skills, and creative abilities to their full potential. The Querent needs to tap into his innate power, even if he is still unaware of much of it, rather than hiding his light under a bushel. Life is opening up and there are choices to be made in order to determine which direction to take. Care should be taken because there may be an element of trickery or manipulation surrounding the Querent. Guidance could come in the form of the Querent's own intuition and innate wisdom, or in the guise of a person who acts as a powerful catalyst for change and transformation.

Fool Proof

At one time the Fool came at the end of the card series. In modern Tarot cards the Fool always represents the number zero and the start of a journey.

INTUITION AND HARMONY

The High Priestess and the Empress can represent either a significant woman or the feminine side of the Querent. The High Priestess is a strong indication of the intuitive side of the Querent's nature, the subconscious and often hidden feelings and gifts. The Empress represents the cyclical nature and harmony of the natural world, and brings to mind its growth and productivity. Physical and emotional well-being is also signified.

Imperious
The High Priestess from the Egipcios Kier Tarot.

Floral
The High Priestess from the Universal Waite Tarot.

III — THE EMPRESS

Strong
Athena is well-known in Greek mythology for her strength and femininity.

III

Copyright © 1981 by Motherpeace

Empress

Regal
The Empress from the Morgan-Greer Tarot.

Relaxed
The Empress from the Motherpeace Tarot.

High Priestess
and Empress

Delving into the occult
*The hidden mysteries of the occult
world are contained in
the symbolism of the cards.*

The High Priestess

This card suggests intuition, psychic
abilities, and spiritual knowledge.
The Querent is entering a learning
phase and will be drawn to things of
an esoteric nature, perhaps through a
dream, a book, or a person that she
meets. That person will appear in the
Querent's life to teach her about the

hidden mysteries of the occult world
and the realms of the unconscious.
The High Priestess also signifies that the
Querent's powers of intuition and insight
will be heightened and that help and
guidance will be provided by what
comes to light. Entering the world of
dreams and symbols has the potential
to offer fresh insights and fascinating
new discoveries about abilities that
the Querent did not even know she
possessed. There are pitfalls, however,
in exploring these untapped aspects of
the psyche and the Querent needs to
use her intuition to differentiate between
truth and deception. If the card is
reversed the Querent becomes less
introspective and is willing to interact
with others to find guidance.

The Empress

The Empress is the earth mother
goddess and as such symbolizes the
abundance of nature, fertility, and
growth. She is a reminder that

everything moves in cycles and ripens in the fullness of time. If this card appears in a spread, it means that the Querent can improve her circumstances by drawing on her own wisdom, strength, and creativity. Something is about to come to fruition and a strong desire will be fulfilled. A creative and productive phase is being heralded and this could manifest itself as, for instance, a marriage, the birth of a child, or perhaps a move to a new house.

This card is very auspicious when the Querent is getting married, creating a home, or becoming a parent, because it suggests that the strong need for emotional well-being will be fulfilled. It is also associated with the enjoyment of the simple pleasures of life. The Empress may appear as a woman who embodies these principles and who can act as a role model for the Querent. Though the Empress represents the earth mother, if reversed the card can suggest maternal rejection.

CONTROL AND ORDER

Both these cards are concerned with the imposition of order. The Emperor signifies inner control, discipline, willpower, and the need for the Querent to have a grip on his own world, and an awareness of the impact he has on others. The Hierophant indicates the need for order and awareness in the Querent's inner self, and contact with the spiritual side of his nature.

Wealthy
The Emperor from the Gypsy Tarot.

THE EMPEROR   L'EMPEREUR

Enthroned
The Emperor from the Visconti Sforza Tarot.

Ancient
The Hierophant from the Haindl Tarot.

Wise
The Hierophant from the Visconti Sforza Tarot.

The Hierophant

Direction
The Emperor and the Hierophant offer the Querent control, order, and direction within a chaotic world.

Emperor and Hierophant

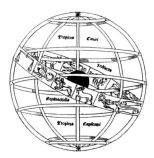

Planetary influences
*Astrological symbolism is often
incorporated in the meaning of
certain cards.*

The Emperor

Drawing this card denotes that the Querent is in a strong and solid position and has the confidence and ambition to realize his goals. The Emperor represents power, self-control, discipline, and a strict code of ethics; selecting it suggests that the Querent is ready to establish himself in the world. This might manifest itself in the form of taking on more responsibility, or starting up a business, or putting new or untried ideas to the test.

It is time for the Querent to act in order to realize his goals and achieve success, and to do this he will need to draw on inner resources and have the courage of his convictions. There might be an opportunity to play a more influential role or to take control of a situation, and this could come through a promotion or an acknowledgement that confers honor and status and a higher standing in the world. This card could signify a person in the Querent's life who is powerful, worldly, authoritative, and possibly dictatorial. He is someone trustworthy, solid, and dependable to whom the Querent can turn for advice and encouragement.

The Hierophant

Originally, this card signified religious guidance. Also known as the Pope, the Hierophant represents spiritual power, inner wisdom, and higher awareness. Its appearance in a spread suggests that the Querent needs to look deep within himself for answers of a spiritual or philosophical nature. He might feel drawn to studying a subject that is based on his growing spiritual awareness in order to achieve a meaningful context to his life.

If the Querent is going through times of difficulty or crisis, this card can sometimes indicate that a teacher, mentor, confidant, or therapist is coming into his life to guide and support him. This guide will be instrumental in helping him to develop a belief system or personal philosophy. He or she will be compassionate, empathetic, and understanding, and will have a profound influence. This card also suggests the need to stay open to the idea of looking at different perspectives rather than automatically taking the tried and tested path when faced with a choice. At all times the Querent should act according to his conscience.

Learning

The Hierophant is linked with education and self-fulfillment. This signifies self-discovery or perhaps a mentor will enter the Querent's life to guide him.

CHOICES AND FORCES

The Lovers denotes that a choice will need to be made, not necessarily of a romantic nature but one that is likely to have far-reaching consequences. The Chariot, too, signifies two forces pulling in opposite directions. Emotion and intellect might suggest different courses of action, but the Querent has to make a decision that she is comfortable with. The challenge is to choose the way that maintains balance.

Courtly love
The Lovers from the JJ Swiss Tarot.

VI

THE LOVERS

6

THE LOVERS

Wild passions
The Lovers from the Golden Dawn Tarot.

Cupid
*This mythical figure is
known for bringing
together lovers.*

Double sphinx
*The Chariot from the
Universal Waite Tarot.*

7

Le Chariot   Il Carro
The Chariot   El Carro
Der Triumphwagen

Horse duo
*The Chariot from
the Barbara
Walker Tarot.*

Lovers and Chariot

The Lovers
This card symbolizes a strong bond such as friendship, partnership, or a marriage.

The Lovers

This is not a card that simply addresses romantic love and partnerships, rather it is a card of change and implies a choice that is neither easy nor straightforward. This could be a choice regarding love, with the Querent being asked to choose between two different people, or between love and a career, or any two things that are incompatible. Often this is an agonizing decision because the Querent is well aware that whatever choice she makes, an element of sacrifice is almost certainly involved. There is also a sense that the consequences of her decision will have a profound impact, and for this reason it cannot be made lightly.

The dilemma of being torn between head and heart is often at the root of this card, but it also suggests that when weighing up the pros and cons, the Querent is more likely to find the "right" answer by listening to her intuition as opposed to her intellect. It may shock the Querent to discover that arriving at a decision may have come through gut feeling as opposed to rational thought. An existing relationship might be tested in such a way that the Querent is made more aware of what it is that she most values, but if the card is reversed it may symbolize that the querent cannot expect a partnership at this time.

The Chariot

The Chariot, sometimes called Victory, symbolizes the need for self-control, discipline, and willpower. The Querent is being challenged to keep opposing forces in balance, while at the same time maintaining stability and equilibrium. This card is often depicted as two horses willfully pulling in different directions, reflecting the fact that the Querent may be struggling with two equally strong but conflicting desires. For instance, she might have a burning ambition to achieve a particular goal, while another part of her personality is fiercely resistant to following that path. She will need all the strength and energy she can muster in order to reconcile the contradictions of her own nature and so resolve the conflict satisfactorily.

Once she is able to make peace with herself, the Querent can move forward and find a more conscious way of directing the course of her own life. This card may also indicate that the Querent will find herself in competition with others, making her more aware of her own competitive instincts. If she can harness these energies and direct them toward a specific goal, she will eventually be successful. A reversed card suggests that the Chariot is not strong enough to control a situation. Recognizing this might ease stress.

FAIRNESS AND REFLECTION

Justice is one of the three cardinal virtues in the Major Arcana (the other two are Strength and Temperance). As its name implies, this card denotes fairness, moderation, and balance. After receiving a verdict or undergoing a resolution of any kind the Querent might want time to reflect on what has happened. The Hermit denotes that a time of quiet reflection is needed for mental and spiritual growth.

Red robes
Justice from the Herbal Tarot.

Success in business and legal matters. Good judgment.

Injustice, legal complications. A great disappointment.

Green gown
Justice from the Astrological Tarot.

Clear-sighted
In law courts Justice is often portrayed blindfolded. In the Tarot she always sees clearly.

Lighting the way
The Hermit from the Haindl Tarot.

The Hermit

Colorful
The Hermit from the Visconti Sforza Tarot.

Justice and Hermit

Justice

This card often illustrates the scales of justice and the sword that cuts through dishonesty and delusion, and imposes a just solution. If this card appears in a spread, the Querent may be facing a difficult decision that has to be weighed carefully before reaching a conclusion. This might involve a legal problem, a court case, or a matter of principle, and suggests that as long as the Querent maintains the courage of his convictions and his integrity, justice will be done. Sometimes a person is at hand to offer help and give advice.

Keeping a well-balanced outlook and taking responsibility for his situation will put the Querent in a strong position and enable him to be decisive and fight for what he believes in. This card often suggests a moral or legal victory, with the Querent feeling vindicated by the just outcome of a matter. If this card is reversed it hints at some kind of injustice so the Querent may need to be wary and search deeper within himself to uncover the truth.

Revealing light
The lantern carried by the Hermit signifies the illumination gained from looking within.

The Hermit

Throughout history hermits have distanced themselves from their surroundings, literally by going into the wilderness, or metaphorically through meditation, in order to free themselves from the trappings of human society. They did this in order to seek spiritual enlightenment.

The Hermit card often signifies that the Querent needs a period of solitude or isolation in order to reflect on his current situation. Meditation, study, and quiet contemplation will help create an atmosphere of inner stillness and quiet, and enable the Querent to grow both spiritually and mentally. If he allows himself to be still and to be introspective much will come to light, and he will discover deeper truths about himself.

If the Querent is wondering which path to follow, time spent alone will give him the space to discover his next course of action intuitively. This solitude might be of his own volition or forced upon him, but whether or not it is out of choice, it has the potential to offer many insights and is a necessary stage of his growth and development. The Querent is also being asked to be patient and recognize the value of slowing down and taking stock of his life. A person who is older and wiser than the Querent might appear to offer counsel and support, but that person will act as a mirror for the wise guide and teacher who is already present within the Querent's own psyche to whom he can turn for inner guidance.

BEGINNINGS AND RESOURCES

The common thread between the cards of Strength and Fortune is change. Life tends to be cyclical but when one period comes to an end and another begins, we sometimes need help to cope with the changes that this brings. While the Wheel of Fortune signifies a new beginning, Strength denotes the physical, mental, and spiritual resources we need to draw on in order to cope with the unknown in the next phase of life.

Snake
The Wheel of Fortune from the Papus Tarot. The snake represents death and destruction.

Anubis
The Wheel of Fortune from the Egipcios Kier Tarot. Anubis is a symbol of rebirth.

Coiled serpent
Strength from the Tarot of the Spirit. The serpent symbolizes sexual magic.

Lion tamer
Strength from the Oswald Wirth Tarot. The lion represents passion.

Fortune and Strength

The Wheel of Fortune

This card is one of the most difficult to interpret since it suggests events that are beyond human control. If this card is drawn it suggests that the Querent has reached the end of a cycle and a new phase is beginning. It brings to mind the cycles of nature, such as the seasons, but these events are out of our hands. Unexpected changes are about to happen, and because they often come unannounced it can feel as if fate has taken a hand in a situation and the Querent has no control.

This can feel either exciting or disconcerting, because there is no certainty as to whether these changes will be positive or negative. They could be related to relationships, work, or home, and can disrupt the patterns of the Querent's life, serving as a reminder that nothing stays the same forever. It may be necessary to let go of the past in order to progress, but the Querent can take comfort in the knowledge that it is sometimes necessary to go down in order to come up again.

Forever turning
The Wheel is a symbol of change and contains the idea of cyclic evolution.

A new opportunity for growth is being heralded and this may come in the form of a person or situation that the Querent is destined to meet. Reversed, the Wheel of Fortune does not predict a bad future, but implies that the Querent is not receptive to change.

Strength

The old name for this card was Fortitude, suggesting determination, physical power, and the stamina to cope with any given situation, no matter how challenging it might be. When the Querent chooses this card it indicates that she will be called to draw upon the courage of her convictions, strength of character, and self-confidence in order to succeed. This could be on a material level, with the Querent putting her plans into action after overcoming certain obstacles, or it might represent spiritual strength as she attempts to come to terms with the more selfish or negative aspects of her character.

This card also represents creative ability and suggests that the Querent is about to tap into her hidden potential. A sudden release of creative energy will have a wonderfully uplifting effect and feel like a new lease of life to the Querent. Becoming more aware of her innate talents and abilities will strengthen the Querent's feelings of self-worth, and belief in her ability to handle herself and the different aspects of her own nature.

If the strength card is reversed it may signify the Querent's determination is tinged with an element of self-doubt.

BLOCKS AND ENDINGS

The ominous picture on the Hanged Man card often makes people afraid, but it denotes a phase in which change is possible, rather than a physical hanging incident. Similarly, the Death card very rarely means a literal death when it appears in a spread but is more likely to signify the end of an era. These cards denote an ending to a phase, but a new beginning is also to be expected.

Woman
The Hanged Man is given a female identity in the Shining Woman Tarot.

The HANGED WOMAN
12

The Hanged Man

Lost in a rainbow
The Hanged Man from the Haindl Tarot.

Dainty
The Hanged Man from the Oswald Wirth Tarot.

Leonine
Death from the Ukiyoe Tarot.

Skeletal
Death from the Thoth Tarot.

Hanged Man and Death

Finding the inner self
*The Hanged Man signifies a
turning point, often toward a
more spiritual life.*

The Hanged Man

This card can often provoke fear,
but in fact it does not indicate
physical punishment or hardship.
The Hanged Man indicates that the
Querent is in limbo and, at least for
the time being, unable to change his
present circumstances. A feeling of
being trapped gives rise to fear,
anxiety, and a deep sense of unease,
and the Querent may be called upon to
sacrifice something he values in order to
move forward. This needs to be done
voluntarily and with the knowledge that
although something will undoubtedly be
lost, something else (perhaps of even
greater value) will be gained that will
ultimately improve his circumstances.

The Querent's consciousness is
expanding and he might experience
some kind of spiritual transformation
even though at the time he might not be
aware of this. It can be a painful time
when the Querent is acutely aware of
what is passing out of his life, and all
he can do is have faith that things will
change for the better. A turning point
has been reached and circumstances
need to be looked at from a different
angle in order to gain a new
perspective. Being patient and reflective
on his position can bring the Querent
illumination, freedom, and peace.

Death

Like the Hanged Man, the Death card
is often feared unnecessarily. Contrary
to what you might imagine, this card

is not indicative of an imminent death. Actually it indicates the passing of an old way of life and suggests that the Querent is about to embark on a new phase. In order to do this, he will need to let go of the past and put it behind him. This might involve the end of a relationship, the loss of a job or way of life, but whatever change is represented by this card, the Querent will need courage to face the fact that he can no longer hold on to the past.

A complete transformation is being offered to the Querent and he could find himself in new surroundings, in a new relationship, or facing a new challenge of some kind. Sometimes this card means a marriage, a job change, or the chance for a fresh start. He might also need to adopt a new attitude in order to move on and take advantage of the new opportunities that are opening up.

If the Death card is reversed it suggests some kind of stasis in the Querent's life, perhaps because he is not open to change.

BALANCE AND FRUSTRATION

Temperance is one of the three cardinal virtues to appear in the Tarot pack, the others being Justice and Strength. The keywords here are balance and moderation. A measured view must be taken before any action. However, the appearance of the Devil may indicate that this approach can make the Querent feel thwarted at every turn. A way needs to be found of overcoming the frustration.

Opposition
The Devil from the Visconti Sforza Tarot.

Moderation
Temperance from the Morgan-Greer Tarot.

Angelic
Temperance cards often make use of celestial imagery in their design.

THE DEVIL

Frustration
The Devil from the Golden Dawn Tarot.

Temperance

Balance
Temperance from the Motherpeace Tarot.

Temperance and Devil

Harmony
*Temperance indicates the
adoption of a more balanced
approach to life.*

Temperance

The Temperance card indicates
that the Querent needs to adopt a
balanced and moderate approach
in relation to both herself and others.
Rather than giving in to her usual
tendency to take an extreme point of
view, or indulging her habit of reacting
too hastily or emotionally to a situation,
the Querent must strive to become
patient and compassionate and must
take the time to explore her feelings.

A strong element of cooperation
is indicated by this card, with the
Querent both giving of herself and
receiving the help of others, and it often
indicates a happy and harmonious
relationship, be it a friendship or a
marriage. If the Querent has been
excessive in any way, the appearance
of Temperance in a spread is
suggesting that she should take herself
in hand and learn to compromise.

This may involve adopting a more
circumspect attitude to finances or
health—perhaps by cutting back on
food or drink and curbing any
extravagant tendencies. Being willing
to change can create a happier and
more balanced way of life.

Reversed, this card may indicate that
the Querent is unable to act in a
moderate way.

The Devil

The Devil often frightens those who are
new to the Tarot but in a reading it is
unlikely to signify evil. The Devil can
represent any situation in which the

Querent feels enslaved or trapped by someone or something. She might be feeling angry, frustrated, or enraged by these uncomfortable circumstances, and yet for whatever reason it might be hard to express these emotions.

It is important that the Querent realizes that although she appears to be stuck in a very negative situation, there is a solution to the problem that she has not yet seen. Once she realizes what is at the root of her difficulty and takes responsibility for it, she will be able to break free of the chains that bind her to it. In order to do this she might have to confront certain characteristics or habits of which she is ashamed or by which she is embarrassed. The challenge for the Querent is to recognize her more negative emotions and to have the courage to break free. Sometimes a person in the Querent's life, who pulls all the strings and has a hold on her, represents these characteristics.

If the Devil card is reversed it indicates that the Querent can find strength to free herself from oppression.

UPHEAVAL AND FUTURE LUCK

Once again, the keyword here is change. The Tower denotes that a dramatic upheaval is about to take place, which might have painful results. It is likely to be a confusing time, but one that could have positive benefits if the chance to make a new start is taken. The Star denotes better luck for the future. It is the light that shows the way forward.

Drama
The Tower from the Ukiyoe Tarot.

Confusion
The Tower from the Universal Waite Tarot.

Lucky star
The Star from the Witches Tarot.

Guiding light
The Star from the Papus Tarot.

Tower and Star

Bolt out of the blue
The Tower represents sudden change that can mark the beginning of a new opportunity.

The Tower

The Tower symbolizes dramatic change, which brings about an unexpected alteration to the Querent's circumstances. Disruptions and setbacks are likely to occur and these could manifest as the end of a relationship, the loss of a job, or any other situation that threatens the Querent's security. The changes that appear often come as a shock, and the upheaval they create can turn everything upside down and upset the status quo completely.

How the Querent responds to these events will to a large extent determine the outcome of this bewildering period. He is being offered the opportunity to reassess his values, lifestyle, and relationships, and to live more in accordance with his true self. This could involve allowing worn-out beliefs to fall away, especially if they have been too rigid or fixed, and adopting a new set of attitudes. It could also mean breaking out of a situation that has become too restrictive and no longer conducive to the Querent's growth. The opportunity for a brand new start is indicated and although certain illusions may have been shattered, this paves the way for the Querent to restructure his life in a more authentic way. The stage is definitely set for a change for the better.

Reversed, the Tower card can indicate chaos of a lesser extent. Alternatively it can mean that the Querent is willing to struggle on amid the ensuing chaos, or that the difficult situation is at least set to continue for a while longer.

The Star

The Star is the card of hope and heralds good fortune and faith in a better future. It can often signify a return to health in a physical, mental, or spiritual sense, and a renewed trust in life.

Perhaps the Querent has been or is currently beset by difficulties; this card denotes that finally the light can be seen at the end of the tunnel. A new life is being shown and because this is the wish-fulfillment card, a happy outcome can confidently be expected. Provided that he holds on to his faith and trusts that he is being guided even in times of hardship, the Querent will soon experience the joy and uplifting feeling engendered by real happiness. On the other hand, if he has been kept in the dark over something or has been struggling to carry on, this card suggests that help is finally on the way.

If the card is reversed it suggests that the Querent's self-belief and optimism may be on the verge of faltering, blocking the path to happiness.

DISCOVERY AND FULFILLMENT

Perhaps more usually thought of as opposites, in the Tarot the Sun and the Moon can both denote fulfillment in some way. The Moon can signify that the Querent is to discover her hidden depths after a time of uncertainty and confusion. The Sun is one of the most auspicious cards in the Tarot and indicates success, joy, and fulfillment, or the achievement of a personal goal.

Discovery
The Moon from the Visconti Sforza Tarot.

18

La Lune

Der Mond **The Moon** La Luna

La Luna

Revelation
The Moon from the Barbara Walker Tarot.

Success
*The Sun from the
Tarot de Marseilles.*

XIX

THE SUN

XIX

THE SUN

Joy
*The Sun from the
Tarot of the Spirit.*

Moon and Sun

Two-faced
The double-sided image of the Moon symbolizes both intuition and deception.

The Moon

When the Moon appears in a reading it indicates that the Querent is entering a period in which she will be more susceptible to intuition and inspiration. At the same time, she is more prone to self-deception, fantasy, and illusion, because nothing is what it seems. It will be hard to separate fact from fiction and this could lead to confusion.

The Querent may feel as if she is groping in the dark and unable to shed any light on her situation. There is a sense of losing direction and this can be accompanied by feelings of depression and hopelessness. If the Querent is prone to irrational fears, these might have very little to do with the actual situation, but will nevertheless feel very real. She could be deluding herself or be the victim of someone else's act of deception. Often there is an undercurrent of deceit that is hard to pin down but which makes dealing with others very confusing.

On a more positive note, this can be a very creative time and one in which the Querent can glimpse hidden aspects of herself through dreams and intuitive insights. It might take time, however, before she is ready to form a clear picture of what she has discovered.

The Sun

The appearance of the Sun in a spread suggests that the Querent is about to achieve a personal goal and enjoy the fruits of her labor. It is one of the most positive cards to be found in the Tarot deck and suggests that the Querent now has the energy and enthusiasm to fulfill her aspirations and that there will be every opportunity to accomplish her ambition. If the Querent has been feeling under par recently, she will begin to feel more confident and energetic, as well as experiencing a growing sense that so much more is now possible and that there is everything to play for.

This card can also herald a period of creativity, greater prosperity, and happiness in personal relationships. It often signifies a happy marriage and contentment in love. The Querent feels optimistic about the future and is ready to move forward and live life to the full. Worldly success is also possible: the Sun card could indicate the Querent being promoted or enjoying greater status and recognition.

Gray Matter

The cabbalist letter for moon meant "back of the head" while the letter for sun meant "whole head," but specifically the brain's "gray matter"—the part that makes us human.

OPPORTUNITY AND REWARD

Being rewarded for one's efforts and the beginning of a new cycle is the inherent meaning of both of these cards. Judgement indicates a coming to terms with one's past in order to move on, while the World card symbolizes the successful conclusion of one phase and the beginning of a positive new phase of growth.

Pharaonic
Judgement from the Egipcios Kier Tarot.

Floating
Judgement from the JJ Swiss Tarot.

Spiked
Judgement card from the Tarot de Marseilles

Universal
The World from the Thoth Tarot.

Circle dance
The World from the Papus Tarot.

Judgement and World

Judgement

The Judgement card indicates letting go of the past and a new lease of life. The Querent will be given the opportunity to take an honest look at his life and to evaluate how true to himself he has been. In order to let go of the old, it might be necessary to come to a point of acceptance and forgiveness of past mistakes and failures, and to release any negative feelings that are preventing the Querent from moving on. Coming to terms with aspects of himself or his past that he has suppressed will be an important part of this process. This card, more than any other, is a reminder that we reap what we sow, and the Querent can look forward to being rewarded for past efforts. This could be on a worldly level, such as a promotion or greater success, or it might manifest as a deep sense of spiritual fulfillment.

There is also a chance to acknowledge untapped potential that has remained dormant, and the Querent might soon find his creativity and spirituality emerging. If the Querent

World vision
The trials and tribulations of the journey of life culminate in fulfilment in the World.

has been ill or depressed, he might enjoy a return to health and experience a rebirth or spiritual awakening.

If the Judgement card is reversed it may suggest that the Querent is unreceptive to the notion that his life has moved on.

The World

As with many of the other Tarot cards, such as the Wheel of Fortune, the World card symbolizes change and indicates the end of one cycle and the beginning of another. It is a very positive card because it suggests achievement and satisfaction. Something has been successfully completed and the Querent is about to be richly rewarded for his efforts. This may take the form of worldly success with a dream coming true, or there could be a feeling of spiritual well-being and a deep sense of inner peace.

Through life's trials and tribulations the Querent has gained a growing self-knowledge and spiritual understanding and has integrated the different aspects of himself into a meaningful whole. He can be justifiably proud of what he has been able to achieve on both a physical and spiritual level. However, this card also suggests that he will soon be embarking on a new cycle that will bring with it the challenges and opportunities for further growth

While this is all positive, a reversal of the card does not necessarily mean failure, but that nothing has exactly been achieved either. It could be that the Querent may be feeling in a state of limbo.

DIVIDING THE MAJOR ARCANA

It is possible to subdivide the Major Arcana into eight categories, each of which describes a different aspect of our experience. It is important to mention that some of these categories overlap and so cards that contain more than one meaning will fall into more than one category.

Responsibility
The second category is called Responsibility to Others and contains the Empress, the Emperor, Judgement, Temperance, and the Lovers.

Enlightenment
The first category is called Inner Power and the cards that belong to this description are the Emperor, the Empress, the Magician, the High Priestess, the Hierophant, the Hermit, and the World.

Living
The third category is entitled Everyday Living. The Empress, Justice, and the Devil all fit into this group.

Reality

Category five is named Cards of Reality and contains the Emperor, the Chariot, Strength, and the Sun.

Fate

The fourth category is called Reacting to Fate and the cards that aptly fit into this category are the Wheel of Fortune, the Hanged Man, Death, the Devil, the Tower, Judgement, the Moon, and the Star.

Dreams

Category seven is called Cards of Dreaming and Doing, and is comprised of Temperance, the Star, and the Chariot.

Black and white

Category six is called Cards of Light and Dark and has the same cards as category four: the Wheel of Fortune, the Hanged Man, Death, the Devil, the Tower, Judgement, the Moon, and the Star.

On the move

The cards that belong in category eight, the Cards of Moving Forward, are the Fool, the Chariot, the Wheel of Fortune, the Sun, Judgement, and the World.

The Four Suits of the Minor Arcana

Minor Arcana
The four suits of Cups, Wands, Swords, and Pentacles from the Tarot de Marseilles.

Each suit has cards from ace to ten, plus four court cards: the Page, the Knight, the Queen, and the King. When interpreting the significance of these cards in a spread, the meaning associated with the element of the suit is considered together with its number or the gender of the court card.

The suit of Cups

The suit of Cups represents situations and emotions that are connected with love, joy, happiness, fulfillment, personal relationships, deep feelings, creativity, and spirituality. It is associated with water and the zodiac signs of Cancer, Scorpio, and Pisces. Through the suit of Cups the Querent becomes more aware of her unconscious motives, learns to trust her intuition, and develops greater emotional maturity.

The suit of Wands

The suit of Wands or Batons represents energy, imagination, enthusiasm, travel, growth, advancement, ambition, hard work, strength in adversity, and ambition. This suit is associated with fire, and the zodiac signs of Aries, Leo, and Sagittarius. Fire acts as a catalyst and can transform our perception of things into something more meaningful.

The suit of Pentacles

The suit of Pentacles (also known as Coins or Disks) signifies material and financial security, and someone who is resourceful, practical, and reliable.

Its associations are earth, and the signs of Taurus, Virgo, and Capricorn. This suit describes the material and physical world, our sense of self-worth and how bound up it is with our possessions and attachments. It also symbolizes achievements and losses, and what we truly value.

The suit of Swords

The suit of Swords is connected to mental and spiritual development, power, action, courage, and obstacles that need to be overcome. Air, Gemini, Libra, and Aquarius are associated with this suit and the double-edged sword epitomizes its duality—the piercing clarity of the rational mind gives greater understanding, but it can also be a sharp cutting weapon that can wound.

Minor Arcana

This set of cards, with its suits, numbers, and picture cards is very similar to a deck of regular playing cards.

THE ACES

The Aces, the first cards in the suits, represent a foundation and a springboard. They signify creative potential, new beginnings, and a time for the Querent to take action. They contain all of the raw and undivided energy and power of the suit to which they belong, and indicate that if the Querent is willing to seize the initiative, they will create new opportunities for growth and change.

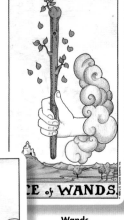

Wands
The Ace of Wands symbolizes the essence of fire.

Cups
The Ace of Cups marks the beginning of a new relationship.

Pentacles

The Ace of Pentacles denotes material success and security.

Swords

The Ace of Swords indicates powerful new ideas and clear thinking.

Four Aces

Energy
*Inspiration, excitement,
and enthusiasm are signified
by the Ace of Wands.*

Ace of Wands

This card represents renewal and a
surge of creative energy that marks
a new beginning. The Querent is filled
with excitement and inspiration and
he might be starting a new project or
formulating a new goal about which
he feels particularly enthusiastic. It is
the beginning of a wonderfully creative
phase and although it will necessitate
hard work to bring the Querent's efforts
to fruition, provided he retains his vision
he will enjoy the journey. A new spiritual
awareness is sometimes experienced.

Ace of Cups

This is an auspicious card for
emotional fulfillment in an existing
or a new relationship because it
symbolizes love, joy, and contentment.
It might indicate a marriage, falling in
love, or the birth of a child. The Querent
is embarking on a happy, positive, and
productive phase of his life, and there is
much to be grateful for. This card can
also mark the awakening of a creative
talent or artistic inspiration, as well as
a growing spiritual understanding.

Ace of Pentacles

Physical and material comfort, well-
being, and a sense of inner worth
based on a solid foundation are all
indicated by this card. The Querent can
expect to feel content with his lot, and
both success and money are in the
offing. This may be a result of his own
efforts or come through a windfall or
legacy. Investment in a new enterprise
or a promotion indicates improved
finances. The Querent has both the

physical energy and the material means to work toward his goals and realize his ambition.

Ace of Swords

This card suggests that change is inevitable on both an inner and an outer level. The Querent experiences a powerful new mental energy that he will need to direct in a controlled and decisive way if he is to meet the challenges that lie before him. Clear thinking and the ability to make rational decisions will help to overcome obstacles, and acting with fairness and integrity will win the day. Sometimes this card indicates a just outcome of a legal matter, despite difficult odds. Often the Querent will find himself acting with more courage and determination than he has ever expressed before.

Playing the Ace Card

The Aces are the basis of each suit and are linked to the cabbalist idea of the Tree of Life (see pages 20–21). We should take note of the special opportunities offered by each card.

THE TWOS

After the power and energy of the Aces, the Twos give the Querent the opportunity to restore the balance and resolve any conflict. Some consolidation might be indicated, although this could also, in the case of the Two of Swords, indicate deadlock. The Twos symbolize duality and the union of opposites. They are the number of harmony and co-operation, and often indicate there is a choice to be made.

Overflowing
*The Two of Cups
from the Thoth Tarot.*

Fiery cross
*The Two of Wands
from the Thoth Tarot.*

Deadlock
*The Two of Swords
from the Thoth Tarot.*

Peace

SWORDS

Change

Yin and yang
*The Two of Pentacles
from the Thoth Tarot.*

Four Twos

Sexual equality
The Two of Cups indicates a good balance of masculine and feminine.

Two of Cups

This card describes the relationship between two people and can indicate a love affair, engagement or marriage, a friendship, or a business partnership. It denotes compatibility, harmony, and emotional balance in a personal or professional relationship, and reconciliation after an argument or separation. It is a good card if the Querent is thinking of starting a relationship, suggesting a loving and trustworthy partner.

Reversal of this card suggests that the Querent may be involved in an imperfect relationship or partnership.

Two of Wands

This card suggests that the Querent is ready to make a decision about what to do next. New opportunities are being offered and she will need to act on her intuition and have the courage to follow her vision. Perhaps she has come so far but now needs to take the initiative in order to realize a goal or ambition. This could involve a career decision, such as forming a new business partnership or embarking on a joint venture. Reversed, she decides to take a new challenge.

Two of Pentacles

The Querent needs to maintain a sense of balance with regard to practical matters and material security, and use her funds and resources to the best of her abilities. She might be challenged with juggling two situations at the same time, and it could take a while before she can manage to do this successfully.

Above all, this card is saying that the Querent has the talent, ability, application, and emotional and physical stamina to start something new and to make a success of it. A reversal of the card indicates that the Querent is finding it increasingly hard to maintain a sense of balance.

Two of Swords

A deadlock or stalemate is often the experience of this card, particularly if the Querent is unable to make a decision because of fear of the consequences. A disagreement or conflict with someone is sometimes indicated, but often it is the Querent who is in conflict with herself over a difficult choice that needs to be made, and as a result she remains stuck. She might be caught in a situation that she is refusing to face, but until she can be honest with herself and clear the air, she will be unable to take action and move on. If the card is reversed she may find that she is more receptive to help from outside sources.

THE THREES

Three is the number of creativity, growth, action, energy, and enthusiasm. The Querent is now in a position to enjoy what has been achieved through the partnerships that were started with the Twos. Any problems that were encountered in the last phase are resolved and the Querent can move ahead into a more expansive stage. Three is an optimistic sign, except for the Three of Swords, which can signify a disappointment.

Action
The Three of Wands from the Morgan-Greer Tarot.

Enthusiasm
The Three of Cups from the Morgan-Greer Tarot.

Energy
*The Three of
Pentacles from the
Morgan-Greer Tarot.*

Clouds on the horizon
*The Three of Swords from the
Morgan-Greer Tarot*

Four Threes

Pierced heart
*Loss, separation, and heartache
are associated with the Three
of Swords.*

Three of Cups

Happiness and good fortune are associated with this card. This could mean that a joyful celebration is indicated, such as a marriage or the birth of a child, or that a wonderfully happy social life is in store. There could be a birth in a symbolic sense, with the Querent beginning something which is close to his heart. A new creative phase promises emotional fulfillment, and any past difficulties can now be resolved. If the Querent has been ill this card can mean healing and a renewal of trust. A disappointment may be in store if the card is reversed.

Three of Wands

Optimism with regard to a new venture is symbolized by this card. The Querent is filled with enthusiasm and inspiration and is ready to begin the next phase of something that has already started. The promise of a successful outcome is indicated, but much hard work and effort is required before it reaches its full potential. However, this is an excellent time for the Querent to promote himself and his talents, because he has the courage of his convictions. If reversed, the card suggests the Querent is hesitant to embark on something new.

Three of Pentacles

The message of this card is that consistent effort will bring fulfillment and success. The Querent needs to use his abilities to the full so that he can capitalize on the initial success that has been achieved. He is now in a position to develop his talents, and to make progress any project on which he has been working. Not only will he be rewarded for his efforts, but he will also be valued for his achievements, and can enjoy the deep satisfaction and pride gained from doing a good job. Reversed, this card suggests the Querent may be indifferent to the task.

Three of Swords

The Querent should prepare himself for a disappointment or upheaval if this card appears in a spread. Something is coming to an end and pain and sorrow often accompany this. The card might mark the breakup of a relationship, a separation, or an acrimonious quarrel, but this is inevitable and necessary in order to clear the way for the future. The Querent needs to be honest with himself so that he can come to terms with this upsetting situation and begin the healing process. Reversed, it shows an unwillingness to confront the upheaval.

THE FOURS
Four is the number of stability, security, structure, and order, which might at first appear to be positive attributes. However, its appearance in a spread can mean different things, depending on the Querent's expectations and situation. It might denote a feeling of contentment, but it could equally suggest dissatisfaction and might indicate that the Querent must undertake much hard work if a new status quo is to be achieved.

Bored boy
The Four of Cups from the Universal Waite Tarot.

Merry maidens
The Four of Wands from the Universal Waite Tarot.

Pensive prophet
The Four of Pentacles from the Universal Waite Tarot.

Stone sleeper
The Four of Swords from the Universal Waite Tarot.

Four Fours

The power of possessions
The Four of Pentacles signifies too great an emphasis on material possessions.

Four of Cups

Relationships are prone to give rise to boredom and dissatisfaction at this time, and the Querent might feel a strong desire for change. There could be feelings of resentment or disappointment, perhaps because the Querent's expectations have not been fulfilled and she feels let down as a result. However, there is an opportunity to make progress, albeit slowly, if the Querent is willing to adopt a new approach, by reevaluating her present circumstances and taking responsibility for the current impasse.

Four of Wands

This card indicates a creative achievement and the Querent can justifiably feel content with her hard-earned success. She is now reaping the fruits of her labor and there is a sense of well-being on both a personal and a professional level. The Querent can enjoy a period of peace and tranquility, perhaps by taking a vacation. After this, she will be inspired to work even harder to achieve her goals.

Four of Pentacles

This card warns against becoming too miserly or acquisitive and hanging on to possessions out of a fear of loss. Holding on too tightly to what she has will cause the Querent to stagnate and stop growing. While material and financial security are important, if the Querent places too much emphasis on these things she is unlikely to achieve the sense of well-being that she is seeking. She is much more likely to feel good about herself when she realizes that her sense of self-worth is not dependent on possessions.

Four of Swords

Often this card suggests that the Querent needs time to be alone in order to rest and recuperate. This could mark a period of convalescence after an illness, or a distressing experience, or a well-deserved rest after a period of hard work. The Querent can enjoy a respite from life's stresses and strains and an opportunity to recharge her batteries. This period of isolation might be chosen or enforced, but even if the latter is the case the Querent will soon recognize that time to herself is a blessing in disguise.

Square Deal

Just as a square has four sides, the Fours put forward the notion of stability and order. But this need not be dull; we all need structure in our lives.

THE FIVES

Five is a number of change and uncertainty. If a Five appears in a Tarot spread it can represent a sense of loss and regret, changeability or versatility. There might be difficulties and obstacles ahead that will need hard work if they are to be overcome—if indeed they can be overcome—and there could be petty problems that cannot be avoided. Skill is needed in order to handle this volatile energy successfully.

Disappointment
The Five of Cups from the Thoth Tarot.

Disappointment

Strife
The Five of Wands from the Thoth Tarot.

Strife

Worry
*The Five of Pentacles
from the Thoth Tarot.*

5

Worry

Defeat
*The Five of
Swords from
the Thoth Tarot.*

5

Defeat

Four Fives

Unlucky in love
*The message of the
Five of Cups could be
a disappointment in love.*

Five of Cups

A sense of disappointment and regret accompanies this card. The Querent might be grieving over the loss of a relationship or because he has made a wrong choice. A quarrel or split with a partner might have taken place, but though things perhaps look bleak, something of value still remains. Rather than feeling sorry for himself and dwelling on the past, the Querent should attempt to recognize

that all is not lost and there is still something to work on for the future. Reversed, the card signifies the Querent is ready to do just that.

Five of Wands

This card suggests that the Querent is prepared to meet the challenge of competing with others, testing his own skills and overcoming obstacles in order to achieve an ambition. This might involve a struggle and he will need to be courageous and patient when dealing with a difficult situation. Nothing runs smoothly and there are likely to be delays or arguments. Care should be taken with any contracts or agreements. A reversed card means the struggle may be ugly, but the more positive meaning of this card is triumph over adversity.

Five of Pentacles

This card signifies loss and hardship. The Querent might lose faith in himself, perhaps because he has suffered a financial loss or feels impoverished in some way. Alternatively, there could be a loss or difficulties in the Querent's emotional life. A solution is available provided he is willing to review his circumstances and realize the need for a new attitude. A fresh start on both an inner level and on a financial level is the promise of this card. When reversed life begins to look better.

Five of Swords

The Querent may find himself powerless to do anything and have no choice but to concede defeat. Facing up to his limitations might be a humiliating experience, but unless he swallows his pride he cannot progress. Focusing on what he can achieve will be productive. Even though this card suggests a loss of some kind, once the situation has been confronted honestly the Querent can move on. Reversed, the card indicates the Querent is ready to make the move.

High Five

The Fives are a difficult set with issues to address such as loss, sadness, and remorse. For case-study examples see p164 and p200.

THE SIXES

Six is the number of balance, harmony, and service. It is associated with the love of home and family and denotes achievement, success, and recognition for effort and hard work, a mixture of contentment with the present and good things in the past. Its appearance in a Tarot spread indicates positive feelings and events: even the Six of Swords denotes moving to better times.

Service
The Six of Wands from the Morgan-Greer Tarot.

Harmony
The Six of Cups from the Morgan-Greer Tarot.

Balance
*The Six of Pentacles
from the Morgan-
Greer Tarot.*

Direction
*The Six of Swords
from the Morgan-
Greer Tarot.*

Four Sixes

Generosity
The Six of Pentacles is the card that represents giving and receiving.

Six of Wands

This is the card of well-deserved success and indicates that the Querent's past efforts are now bearing fruit. It suggests triumph and victory after a struggle, as well as the enjoyment of recognition and reward for hard work. The Querent might hear some good news. For example, finances could get a boost as a result of a promotion or some other positive change. It is time to celebrate.

Six of Pentacles

The Querent's faith in human nature is being restored and she will have a renewed trust in life. This is the card of giving and receiving, and the more benevolent and generous the Querent is to others, the more she will benefit herself. A debt of some kind might be paid or the Querent might offer someone financial support or be on the receiving end of someone's generosity. There is a feeling of abundance and the Querent will delight in sharing her resources with others. She could meet someone who believes in her talents,

Six of Cups

The Querent might be feeling nostalgic and reminiscing about past happiness. A lover or old friend might reappear to help in some way. Sometimes a long-held wish comes true or something that the Querent has worked for brings a reward. A creative talent might be used. It is time to make the best of what the Querent has now and combine it with the positive aspects of her past.

reflecting the Querent's recognition of her own abilities. Greater stability can be enjoyed.

Six of Swords

This card suggests that the Querent will soon be moving away from a stressful situation. Difficulties and problems are being resolved or overcome and the Querent is coming into a calmer and more peaceful period. Although not everything will resolve itself overnight, things are definitely getting better and the future is looking brighter. Sometimes a move or an important journey represents the end of a sad or anxious time.

The Sixes and the Tree of Life

Medieval cabbalists believed that God created the world through ten emanations of pure energy called *Sephiroth*. To help their meditations they contructed visual diagrams of the ten emanations, the most popular of which was the vertical Tree of Life structure. In this diagram the Sixes are central to the Tree of Life.

THE SEVENS

Seven is the number of wisdom, philosophy, spirituality, and psychic abilities. Many cycles in nature correspond to the number seven and it can indicate the end of a cycle or the completion of a phase. There are choices to be made and decisions to be taken now. Tension between the creative imagination and harsh reality creates a challenge that is overcome with skill, willpower, determination, and courage.

Acuity
The Seven of Wands from the Universal Waite Tarot.

Spiritual riches
The Seven of Cups from the Universal Waite Tarot.

Philosophical attitude
The Seven of Swords from the Universal Waite Tarot.

Abundant harvest
The Seven of Pentacles from the Universal Waite Tarot.

Four Sevens

Seven of Swords
This suggests the need to employ guile and tact to deal with a difficult situation.

Seven of Cups

The Querent's imagination is very active and so much now seems possible. The Querent will be called upon to choose between various options. It is important to separate which ideas are realistic and worth pursuing and which are mere fantasy, and to be as honest as he can with himself about what is within reach. This might not be obvious and the Querent will need to be practical and circumspect when deciding which option to pursue. If the card is reversed it suggests he is willing to take the necessary steps to make his decision a reality. If the correct choice is made, there is much potential for happiness.

Seven of Wands

The Querent might be facing some kind of test that necessitates skill, courage, and determination on his part. Although this will not be easy, he is equipped to cope with this challenge and will win through against the odds. There might be competition from others and although the Querent will have to work hard, he will eventually reap the rewards. Creative pursuits are favored and there could be a change of job or profession coming up. If the card is reversed it may mean the Querent does not have the courage to face up to the test.

Seven of Pentacles

Although the Querent can be proud of his achievements, he cannot afford to rest on his laurels. The results he is hoping for will come through, keeping his goal in sight. If the Querent suffers a setback now, it will be overcome if he remains persistent and focused. Similarly, if there are any decisions to be made, the Querent will need to think them through very carefully before acting. Patience and firm commitment will ensure sustained growth, but if the card is reversed the Querent may end up agitated and dissatisfied.

Seven of Swords

This card emphasizes the need for guile, tact, and diplomacy in order to face a difficult situation or attain an objective. Although adopting such a strategy might leave the Querent with an uncomfortable feeling, it is necessary; a direct confrontation would be counterproductive. If the Querent is facing powerful opposition, he will need to act in a skillful and intelligent way to avoid a collision. He also needs to be vigilant to avoid being deceived. A reversal suggests the Querent is willing to be prudent.

THE EIGHTS

Eight is one of the most powerful numbers of all and symbolizes regeneration, transformation, and positive change. It signifies material success, worldly prosperity, as well as spiritual power, and the balancing of opposing forces. When an eight appears in a spread, the Querent is facing a time of upheaval in her personal or professional life, or on a spiritual level, that might not feel welcome until it is explained.

Under the rainbow
*The Eight of Wands
from the Thoth Tarot.*

Regeneration
*The Eight of Cups
from the Thoth Tarot.*

Indolence

Swiftness

Transformation
*The Eight of Pentacles
from the Thoth Tarot.*

Spiritual power
*The Eight of Swords
from the Thoth Tarot.*

Four Eights

Indecision
*The Eight of Swords signifies
a longing to break free but
a fear of the consequences.*

Eight of Cups

This card indicates change and upheaval. A relationship may be coming to an end and knowing that there is nothing that she can do to change this leaves the Querent feeling depressed or disillusioned. It is necessary to let go of something that is no longer working, even though this involves painful decisions. The Querent recognizes that no further growth is possible without a new beginning.

Reversed, the card indicates she may be better to go along with her particular set of circumstances.

Eight of Wands

After a period of delay the Querent is now entering an exciting and lively period. Things are starting to move and the Querent is filled with energy and enthusiasm for the project in hand. This could imply foreign travel, moving home, or good news from abroad. Alternatively, it could herald a very busy time at work with lots of mental activity. Whatever the Querent initiates now will quickly grow in momentum and anything that she has already worked hard on will begin to take off. If the card is reversed there may be delays.

Eight of Pentacles

The Querent feels a deep sense of personal satisfaction from putting her talents and abilities to good use. She might be developing or perfecting her skills, or discovering a new talent that could lead to an emotionally and financially rewarding profession. The Querent is ready to develop her innate potential. Through hard work, effort, and combining practical skills with creative ability, the Querent will establish a solid foundation to her work and enjoy a new lease of life, no matter what her age. A reversed card suggests the Querent is frustrated that her skills are not achieving the success she desires.

Eight of Swords

The Querent longs to break free from a difficult situation or limiting circumstances, but cannot see a way out. She might be afraid of taking any action because of the consequences. There might be a lot of conflict around her that she is hesitant to confront, and so she becomes trapped by her own indecisiveness. The situation might not be as difficult as she thinks, but she will need to face it as honestly as she can in order to move on, even if it means creating a stir. She may realize that she is responsible for the current dilemma. If the card is reversed her solution becomes clear.

THE NINES

Nine is the number of humanitarian concerns, perfection, and transcendent love. The question of satisfaction and the yearning to move ahead is relevant whenever a Nine appears in a spread. Both the Nine of Cups and the Nine of Pentacles are auspicious cards and signify the highest attainment of an ideal, but the Nine of Swords and the Nine of Wands are far more challenging.

Satisfaction
The Nine of Cups from the Morgan-Greer Tarot.

Progress
The Nine of Wands from the Morgan-Greer Tarot.

Humanitarian concerns

The Nine of Swords from the Morgan-Greer Tarot.

Love

The Nine of Pentacles from the Morgan-Greer Tarot.

Four Nines

Nine of Pentacles
*Well-being, contentment, and
a strong sense of self-worth
are described by this card.*

Nine of Cups

This is the wish card of the Minor
Arcana and promises the fulfillment
of a desire. True happiness and
contentment in love are indicated and
this is a very auspicious card if the
Querent is getting married or making an
emotional commitment. Emotional and
material stability will allow the Querent
to feel at peace with himself and the
world. If a decision needs to be made,
the Querent should follow his heart, but

if the card is reversed the Querent can
look beyond mere contentment to find
an even deeper level of happiness.

Nine of Wands

This is the card of courage and
determination to succeed, no matter
what opposition or obstacles lie ahead.
The Querent is in a strong position from
which to move forward because he
intuitively knows that he is equipped to
face the challenges ahead. He needs
to prepare himself for a setback in the
pursuit of his goal and recognize that
he has strength in reserve to stay the
course. If the card is reversed this
strength may falter.

Nine of Pentacles

The Querent has worked hard and
can now reap the benefits. He can
justifiably take pride in his achievements
and know that he has earned the deep
sense of well-being and contentment.
There is a strong sense of the
uniqueness and value of what he has to
offer and an appreciation of his skills.

The fact that he is not reliant on the approval of others in order to know his worth gives him a feeling of strength and security. A reversal of this card may indicate a recklessness in reaping the benefits of his work.

Nine of Swords

A sense of anxiety and despair accompany this card. The Querent might be having bad dreams or negative thoughts and this anguish can lead to stress and depression. Experiencing guilt for something that has happened can create a sense of foreboding. Sometimes this card indicates suffering in the past which the Querent is unable to forget.

These fears can become a self-fulfilling prophecy and the Querent needs to realize the part they are playing in creating his present reality. That way he will soon realize that his situation is not as bleak as he has imagined. If the Querent has been ill or suffered a loss, he will soon recover and his faith will be renewed.

THE TENS

Ten is the number of completion and marks the end of one cycle and the beginning of another, bringing the wisdom of the experiences that we have gained in the previous cycle. The way in which the cards reflect this differs. The Ten of Cups and the Ten of Pentacles indicate fulfillment, while the Ten of Wands and the Ten of Swords signify difficulties that can be surmounted.

Problems
The Ten of Wands from the Universal Waite Tarot.

Contentment
The Ten of Cups from the Universal Waite Tarot.

Fulfillment
The Ten of Pentacles from the Universal Waite Tarot.

Challenges
The Ten of Swords from the Universal Waite Tarot.

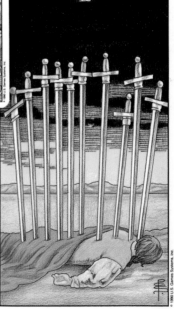

Four Tens

Ten of Wands

This card describes a situation where one is weighed down by burdens and responsibilities.

Ten of Cups

Lasting happiness, contentment, and the realization of the Querent's heartfelt wishes are symbolized here. She is surrounded by the love of friends and family and can now enjoy emotional and spiritual harmony and fulfillment. There may be a joyful event or a situation that signifies the culmination and fulfillment of a dream. A reversed card suggests she might not realize how happy she actually is.

Ten of Wands

This card denotes taking on too much and being weighed down by too many responsibilities. The Querent will soon be able to start a new creative phase, but only once she has let go of the worn-out attitude that is holding her back. It is important that the Querent recognizes her motives for overdoing it, and she might need to lower her expectations while still keeping her goal in sight. A reversal suggests she does not realize she is overdoing it so she feels oppressed.

Ten of Pentacles

A period of contentment and a happy, secure way of life is indicated by this card. The Querent has completed something and she can now enjoy both emotional and material security. There is a feeling of abundance and comfort. This is the card of the family and indicates joyful family gatherings and the feeling of belonging. The Querent might be starting a family or setting up a business that will benefit others in the future. Sometimes this signifies that the

Querent will come into money through an inheritance. A reversed card might mean she is dissatisfied with the security and seeks a challenge.

Ten of Swords

This card indicates the end of a painful situation and the Querent might be feeling at her lowest ebb. Separation and a deep sense of personal loss are the cause of much unhappiness, but although these are difficult to deal with, the Querent will soon begin a new phase and things will start to improve.

Indulging in negative thinking at this time will exacerbate the situation and even though the Querent might feel emotionally spent, she needs to muster the courage to rise from the turmoil and start all over again.

If she can accept the situation as it is, although it is depressing, she will find the strength to overcome this crisis and will eventually emerge stronger and more capable because of it. A reversal of this card suggests the Querent is already at the stage of acceptance.

THE PAGES

The Page (sometimes known as the Prince) is the first of the court cards and can denote either a situation or a person in the Querent's life. If it describes a situation, it is one that is very new or just beginning. If a person is being represented, it is usually a child or a new aspect of the Querent's personality that is emerging. All four of the Pages correspond to the element of earth.

Winged warrior
*The Page of Cups
from the Thoth Tarot.*

Prince of Cups

Spiky spirit
*The Page of Wands
from the Thoth Tarot*

Prince of Wands

Prince of Disks

Powerful player
*The Page of Pentacles
from the Thoth Tarot.*

Prince of Swords

Green giant
*The Page of Swords
from the Thoth Tarot.*

Four Pages

Hidden talents
The Page of Wands indicates creative potential waiting to be realized.

Page of Cups

This card represents a new birth of some kind. The Querent may discover a latent skill that is ready to be developed, or embark on a new course of study. There is a sense of renewal on an emotional level and the Querent might be feeling able to trust love again after a period of hurt and rejection. Love of self as a prerequisite for loving others is also indicated. A person represented by this card will be kind, loving, and in a position to help the Querent in some way, or it could describe a sensitive and artistic child.

Page of Wands

This card often indicates the Querent's untapped creative potential. Good news and exciting new opportunities are in the offing and the Querent might have a flash of inspiration that will guide him. The Querent will need to invest time and energy if new possibilities are to lead to success. If this card represents a person, he will be energetic, impulsive, and enthusiastic.

Page of Pentacles

If the Querent is patient, diligent, and hardworking he will make slow but steady progress and his efforts will eventually pay off. There may be a small improvement to the Querent's finances or the prospect of a promotion. Alternatively, he might be embarking on a training course or period of study in order to enhance his career prospects. He could meet someone who is

practical, reliable, and articulate and whose love of learning acts as a catalyst for new ideas. This person might be in a position of influence.

Page of Swords

The Querent might soon find himself in a situation that will require him to make sure that he has his wits about him before making any decisions. A healthy degree of caution may be advisable because someone may wish the Querent harm or, at the least, may not have his best interests in mind. This card also indicates unexpected news that will open up new opportunities in the Querent's life, but he should at all times proceed with caution. If this card represents a person he will be intelligent, devious, unpredictable, and independent-minded.

Page Boys

The Pages, or Princes, can represent emotional states or actual character types. Specific people can often be identified by examining their characteristics.

THE KNIGHTS

The appearance of one of the Knights in a spread can represent either a situation or a person. If it is a situation, it will involve action, movement, and progress. If it represents a person, it will be someone who is youthful, questing, and active. The likelihood is that something or someone new could be about to enter the Querent's life. All four Knights correspond to the element of fire.

Go-ahead
The Knight of Wands from the Thoth Tarot.

Knight of Cups

Questing
The Knight of Cups from the Thoth Tarot.

Knight of Wands

Active
*The Knight of Swords
from the Thoth Tarot.*

Knight of Swords

Knight of Disks

Progressive
*The Knight of
Pentacles from
the Thoth Tarot.*

Four Knights

Progress
*The Knight of Pentacles
indicates that patience and steady
progress will lead to success.*

Knight of Cups

This card indicates that something new is on the horizon. A proposal of some description is being offered and the Querent will need to consider the practical implications before committing herself. Romance is in the air and the Querent might find herself falling in love with someone who is sensitive, idealistic, and imaginative. Alternatively, she might be identified with these characteristics herself.

Knight of Wands

Travel and moves are symbolized by this card. The Querent might be going abroad either on vacation or on a more permanent basis, or perhaps moving home. There is a feeling that something better is just around the corner. The spirit of adventure is about to enter the Querent's life and she is ready to go into the unknown. If the Querent meets someone whose nature is represented by this card, that person is likely to be charming and fun, but rather volatile and unreliable. Nevertheless, he may inspire her to do something new and adventurous.

Knight of Pentacles

This card signifies slow but steady progress. It might seem as if the Querent is not getting very far or has even come to a standstill, but provided that she is patient and methodical she will eventually reach her goal. Although life may seem rather dull at the moment, she can look forward to being financially rewarded for her efforts and pleased with the results. Someone who is dependable, responsible, and hard-working may come into the Querent's life and help further her ambition.

Knight of Swords

This card often indicates a sudden need to make a drastic change. The Querent might acquire a new perspective that opens up her horizons and motivates her to try something unknown and different. However, the card also carries a warning against being overly impulsive or impatient since this could wreak havoc. If the Querent is facing a difficult situation, she will need to handle the problem head-on and take a firm line. The Knight of Swords often appears as a strong ally who can help the Querent resolve a conflict or overcome an obstacle.

Sense of Adventure

As you might expect, the Knights tend to characterize youthful go-getters, full of energy and eager to seek out adventures or new challenges.

THE QUEENS

These represent important women in the Querent's life. Alternatively, they can symbolize an aspect of the Querent's personality that is apparent or of significance at the time of the reading. This applies to men as well as women. In a female Querent's card spread, a Queen is likely to represent the Querent herself. All the Queens correspond to the feminine element of water.

Shell queen
The Queen of Cups from the Morgan-Greer Tarot.

QUEEN OF RODS

QUEEN OF CUPS

Sunflower queen
The Queen of Wands from the Morgan-Greer Tarot.

Oak tree queen
The Queen of Pentacles from the Morgan-Greer Tarot.

Rose queen
The Queen of Swords from the Morgan-Greer Tarot.

Four Queens

Distant
*The Queen of Swords
is intelligent and quick-thinking
but can be emotionally cut off.*

Queen of Cups

The Queen of Cups has a highly developed intuitive nature and is in tune with her inner world. She might also possess psychic skills. Her loving nature and sensitivity to others makes her a wonderful friend, and she will often be a source of support for others. If the Querent chooses this card it indicates that he has a need to develop a deeper relationship with his inner self. He might be getting more in touch with his feelings.

Queen of Wands

The Queen of Wands is a sociable, warm, open-hearted, loyal, and independent woman. She is also extrovert, generous, popular, and her sympathetic nature draws many to confide in her. She uses her intuition in both her personal and her professional life and is a capable homemaker and businesswoman. This card in a spread suggests that the Querent is ready to express the same qualities.

Queen of Pentacles

The Queen of Pentacles is practical, capable, and self-reliant. She is very hard-working and enjoys the comfort and security of a good income. Although she may be materialistic, she can also be generous to others. She is as happy at home as she is in her career. This card suggests that the Querent might get the opportunity to earn more money or achieve something of real value; or he might meet a woman who facilitates this process and acts as a strong source of support.

Queen of Swords

The Queen of Swords is strong, intelligent, and rather aloof. In spite of, or because of, her strength and detachment, she can sometimes feel emotionally cut off and lonely. Traditionally this card represents a widow, or a woman who is divorced or prefers to be independent.

The Queen of Swords might defend herself against being vulnerable and have impossibly high expectations that serve to keep others at a distance. Her strengths lie in her cool, quick-thinking mind, and resolute and determined nature, but she can be intolerant and judgemental. If the Querent is identified with these characteristics, he might need to let go of certain limiting beliefs and allow other people to help him when he is in need.

Maturity

The Queens are mature and self-possessed. The Querent may try to think of someone they know with these qualities or they may be facets of the Querent themselves.

THE KINGS

The Kings represent either men who are important to the Querent or an aspect of the Querent's personality that needs to be developed, harnessed, or controlled. The King of any suit is a powerful card, with varying character traits coming to the fore. If the Querent is male, a King may represent the Querent's own personality. All the Kings are identified with the masculine element of air.

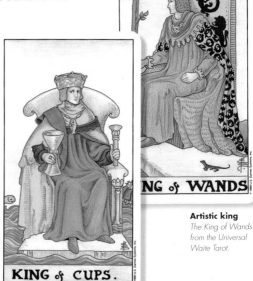

Devious king
The King of Cups from the Universal Waite Tarot.

Artistic king
The King of Wands from the Universal Waite Tarot.

Mystical king
The King of Pentacles from the Universal Waite Tarot.

KING of PENTACLES

KING of SWORDS.

Puritan king
The King of Swords from the Universal Waite Tarot.

Four Kings

Wise man
The King of Cups is a skilled empathist, and is possibly a teacher or counselor.

King of Cups

This man is kind and friendly but slow to demonstrate his affection and adept at hiding his emotions. However, he is very skilled at empathizing with others, possibly in the role of teacher or counselor. This card indicates that the Querent might receive good advice or healing from someone. It may also represent a part of the Querent's character that needs to be developed—she might need to learn to be more open and to trust her feelings.

King of Wands

The King of Wands is a confident, enthusiastic, and strong-willed man who has the ability to inspire and motivate others. He has the courage of his convictions, and because he is a good communicator, he can successfully promote himself and his ideas. His integrity and capacity for leadership make him trustworthy and dependable, and he often acts as a mediator. He will often initiate a project but get someone else to do the donkey work. If the Querent is starting a new enterprise or making exciting changes in her life, she can draw on the positive qualities of this card to help her succeed.

King of Pentacles

The King of Pentacles is a very good-natured and loyal man who values stability and security. He is hard-working and enjoys the material benefits of his labors. He is more practical than intellectual, but he is a man of his word and well-respected. He is often a good businessman and adept with finances. This card bodes well for any business venture and the Querent's financial situation. Greater recognition for the Querent's abilities will bring greater self-confidence.

King of Swords

Intelligent, powerful, ethical, and analytical are some of the characteristics associated with this man. He likes to be in a position of authority and is independent by nature, not liking any restrictions imposed on him. He has learned to control his emotions and will approach a situation in a very logical, rational way. He has an innovative mind and can offer the Querent a strategy when facing a difficult situation. The Querent might be ready to look at something from a new perspective that will lead to professional advancement.

King for a Day

As the final card in the suit, a King represents maturity and wisdom gained from past experience. The King may represent facets of a male or female Querent.

TAROT IN ACTION

Learning the Tarot is like learning a new language, and it takes time to become fluent in reading the cards and understanding their full meaning. The best way of developing your knowledge is by doing sample readings. All systems of divination work through the understanding of patterns. ∿ When learning Tarot, it takes a leap of faith to accept that the cards that the Querent chooses at a particular moment will form a pattern that will tell him something meaningful about his life. ∿ Nobody knows for sure why the pattern between the cards and the Querent's reality reflect each other so beautifully. It is part of the Tarot's inherent mystery.

Preparing to Consult the Cards

It is important to set the stage for a Tarot reading and create the right atmosphere. A Tarot reading is a way of bringing unconscious impressions and intuitive feelings and insights to light, and to do this it is necessary to still the conscious mind. If either the Reader or the Querent is agitated or in an emotionally fraught state, it will be difficult to focus on the reading. Simple rituals such as lighting incense or saying a prayer will help you to enter a receptive and meditative state and to create an ambience that is conducive to a consultation. Observing certain rituals also helps to provide a formal context for the reading. Starting a consultation with an ordered and established routine provides a secure framework in which to work.

Setting the scene

When doing a Tarot reading it is best if you are alone with the Querent in a quiet room so that there are no outside

Preparation
Spend a few moments attuning yourself before starting a reading.

distractions. Spend a few moments attuning yourself before starting the reading and perform whatever ritual practices make you most comfortable and create the right atmosphere for you to work. Some people choose to "go within" for a few minutes so that they can open themselves to their own spiritual guidance. There are many meditation techniques you can use or you can make up one of your own.

Creating a comfortable space

Make sure that you are sitting comfortably before starting a reading. You can sit or kneel on the floor and place the cards on a low table or sit at a table. The table needs to be large enough to spread out all of the cards you are using, as well as having enough room for anything else that you would like to place on it.

A bowl of petals in water, a selection of crystals or anything else that has a special meaning for you can be suitably arranged on the table, but the overall look of the table should not be cramped or cluttered. If you use a black silk cloth to wrap your cards in, this will also serve as an ideal surface on which to lay out the cards.

Tarot Rituals

For further tips on how to prepare for a Tarot reading consult pages 28–33. It is not vital to perform a set ritual but it can help you focus and clear your mind.

THE SIGNIFICATOR

Some Tarot Readers select a card known as the Significator that represents the Querent. This is usually a court card chosen on the basis of the Querent's coloring or astrological sign, but can also be picked at random. This card can then be placed to one side or laid out as part of the spread, and is often used to help the Reader center herself for the reading. One disadvantage of preselecting a card is that it removes one card from the deck that might have been more meaningful if it had come up spontaneously in the reading.

Random choice
The Significator can also be chosen at random.

Significator
When choosing this, it can either be a court card or have an astrological correlation.

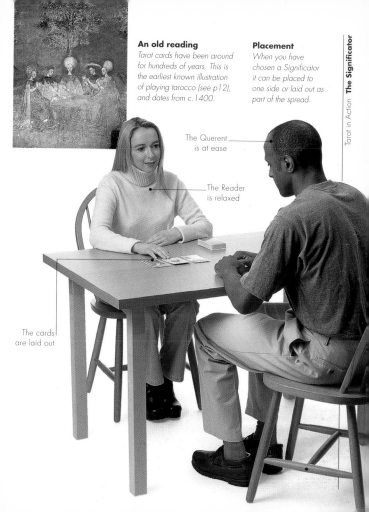

An old reading
Tarot cards have been around for hundreds of years. This is the earliest known illustration of playing tarocco (see p12), and dates from c.1400.

Placement
When you have chosen a Significator it can be placed to one side or laid out as part of the spread.

The Querent is at ease

The Reader is relaxed

The cards are laid out

Putting Questions to the Tarot Cards

Guidance
It is helpful to have a question in mind when you go for a Tarot reading.

It is sometimes helpful for the Querent to ask a question of the cards. This can either be kept private or revealed to the Reader, but it should address only one issue. Sometimes a reading will address a totally different question to the one asked. Often this is because the Querent is unaware of, or afraid to confront, this subject. Fortunately the cards will generally offer helpful insights and guidance on how to deal with this.

The questions to ask

Some layouts are good for general questions, such as an overview of the Querent's present circumstances, while others work well with specific questions. Avoid questions that demand a yes/no answer, or questions such as, "When will I meet the person of my dreams?" or "How long will I have to wait until I'm promoted?" Instead, ask more open questions, such as, "What are the issues or problems surrounding…?", "How can I best overcome these problems?" or "What is the best way for me to…?"

Answering the Querent's questions

Never present information to the Querent as the absolute truth or suggest that an event or state of mind does not involve any choice. The Tarot gives a perspective on a situation but does not, as many people believe, determine a fixed outcome or have all the answers. Even if the reading implies difficulties or unhappiness, suggest to the Querent that this might be a necessary part of the process and a resolution will be found once she has understood the meaning of the experience. Looking at the overall meaning of the cards will usually offer clues to the underlying reason for the present circumstances.

Using a worksheet

In addition, it is a good idea to devise a worksheet for yourself so that you can keep a note of your readings. You can also note the meaning of each card, and as your knowledge of the cards increases, add your interpretations of each card. Experiment with different ways of doing this until you find a method that you are comfortable with.

Question Time

Tarot readings do not offer definitive answers. The relationship between the Reader, Querent, and cards is a complex one and offers information to enable them to make decisions.

SHUFFLING THE CARDS
Before you begin, shuffle the cards well. If you are not using reversed meanings, it is best to keep the cards upright as you do this. Give the deck to the Querent to shuffle and ask him to think of a question as he does so. Then ask him to cut the pack into three piles, and place them face down. Cutting the cards is generally done with the left hand since this connects with the intuitive side of the brain. Next ask the Querent to put the three piles together before handing them back to you.

Mix-up
Make sure the cards are well shuffled and the deck is spread thoroughly.

Pile-up
Bring the cards together and let the Querent cut the deck in three using his left hand.

Lucky star

The Star provides hope in the midst of adversity. It is a portent of true happiness to come.

XVII

THE STAR

Top-up

Using the left hand, place the bottom pile in the middle, then put both piles on top of the first.

Determining the Cards' Significance

Notebook

Make a note of the cards and study how they interrelate.

If you are using reversed meanings it is important that the cards are kept the same way up as they are handed to you, or the reading will be upside down. You then deal the appropriate number of cards from the top of the deck and lay them out face down according to the pattern of the particular spread that you are doing. You can then turn them one at a time

face up, being careful to turn them from side to side and not end to end, which would reverse them.

If you are not using reversed meanings you should turn the cards that have accidentally been reversed to their upright position. If the Querent is sitting opposite to you, the Reader, the cards should appear upright to you.

Taking an overview

When you begin a reading, study all of the cards in a spread and see how they relate to each other as a whole. Get a feel of the general tone of the reading: is there a feeling of happiness and growth or disappointment and difficulties? How many Major Arcana cards are there? Does one particular suit dominate? As you examine the cards in more detail, allow your intuition to draw out the meaning of each card that is most relevant to the reading. As you look at how the cards lie together, compare and contrast them and show the Querent how they interrelate, how the past connects to the here-and-now, and whether the general trend is up or down.

Drawing conclusions from the cards

Synthesizing the cards is quite challenging at the beginning, since there are so many factors to take into consideration. Often the initial impression you have of a card or reading will differ from your final conclusion, and equally the meaning of one card might change when you see how it fits into the overall pattern of the reading. Try to sum up the main points of the reading for the Querent. This will also help you familiarize yourself with the meaning of the cards.

Which Spread?

Different spreads are used for different purposes. Try some sample spreads to see which one works best for you or choose the one with which you are most comfortable.

THE THREE-CARD SPREAD

The three-card spread is used to answer a specific question. The Querent is asked to shuffle and cut the deck and then pick three cards at random. These cards are laid out in a row, the first indicating the past, the second the present, and the third the future. You can also use the three-card spread to determine the day ahead, with the cards representing morning, afternoon, and evening.

PAST PRESENT   FUTURE

Time for change

The Four of Cups reveals the fact that boredom and dissatisfaction with the status quo have precipitated a reevaluation. The Eight of Wands in the present suggests that a new and exciting phase of life is opening up, and The Two of Cups indicates the possibility of a new relationship being formed in the future.

PAST   PRESENT   FUTURE

Excitement ahead

The Ten of Wands means exhaustion after taking on too much and a need to take stock of what has led to this situation. This is underlined by The Hermit, which denotes a time for quiet reflection in order to gain a better understanding. The Knight of Wands indicates that a new creative phase is in the offing and there is something exciting to look forward to.

PAST   PRESENT   FUTURE

Happy horizon

The Emperor suggests that the Querent
has focused on worldly concerns and
achieving her ambitions. The Nine of
Swords in the present, however,
indicates that there is a lot of mental
anguish that threatens to undermine her
sense of achievement. Fortunately, The
Sun promises that the darkness will be
dispelled and happiness and success
will be the outcome.

PAST   PRESENT   FUTURE

Make a sacrifice

A past opportunity to realize a goal is
indicated by the Two of Wands, but
the Chariot appearing in the present
indicates a conflict as to which
direction to take. The Eight of Cups
denotes that a sacrifice of some kind
may be required before a new phase
can begin.

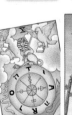  

Case study
*This three-card spread
was drawn by Michael
(see page 156).*

3-Card Reading: Michael

Career query
Michael wanted information about a possible change of career.

Michael, aged 27, was concerned about the prospect of changing careers. He was working in sales but was feeling increasingly drawn to a career in healing and was interested in training as an acupuncturist. He had not discussed this with anyone because he was worried about what people would think. He was earning good money and would have to change his lifestyle dramatically if he decided to become a student again and retrain. He drew the following three cards.

Card one—Wheel of Fortune

This card suggested that Michael had indeed reached the end of a cycle and was ready to make a complete change. There had obviously been some trepidation as to whether this would be a positive or negative change since it was a radical departure from his current situation. He had a strong feeling that this change of career was fated and that in some inexplicable way it was his destiny to become a healer, which was certainly borne out by this particular card. He was definitely being presented with an opportunity to grow, even though he would initially find the prospect rather daunting, especially since he would have to let go of what he was most familiar with.

Card two—Seven of Wands

This indicated a change of job. It also highlighted the challenge that he would be taking on by leaving the security of his job and embarking on a completely new career. He would encounter competition from others and would have

to work hard to prove himself. It hinted
that he would have to contend with stiff
opposition to his decision from friends
or family. There was every indication
that he was equipped to meet the
challenges involved, though hard work
was required to realize his ambition.

Card three—the Magician

The Magician perfectly portrayed the
latent talents and abilities that Michael
had yet to develop. Drawing this card
encouraged him to promote himself and
embark on a career path that would
give him the opportunity to develop.
In spite of the challenges that lay
ahead, he had the self-confidence and
determination to move on and develop
his untapped potential. Michael had
reached an important turning point in
his life and the choices he made would
set the pattern for the future. He would
be greatly helped in the decision-
making process if he followed his own
intuition and self-knowledge and did not
allow himself to be manipulated by
other people's agendas.

THE SIX-CARD SPREAD

This spread uses only the Major Arcana cards and is best consulted for important issues or to answer a vital question. Shuffle the cards and ask the Querent to cut them into three piles face down. Turn the three piles face up, removing the top three cards from each pile and placing them in a row, left to right. Then ask the Querent to pick the next top three cards and create a second row.

Jane, aged 40, came for a reading to ask for guidance on her relationship dilemma. She had had a series of short-term relationships, none of which had been satisfying or fulfilling. She felt that this had a lot to do with the fact that she did all the giving and was taken for granted. Her current relationship was very new and already they were encountering serious difficulties. Soon after they had met, her partner had become moody, demanding, and possessive. She was hoping that the reading would throw some light on why she kept running into the same problems with men.

1
The
Querent

2
Heart of
the Matter

3
Helpful
influences

4
The
Unexpected

5
Unconscious
desires

6
Conceivable
outcome

The Six-card spread
Reader and Querent interact
to produce the spread.

THE HERMIT

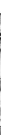

THE TOWER

STRENGTH

THE LOVERS

THE HIEROPHANT

TEMPERANCE

Case study
*This six-card spread was drawn
by Jane (see page 160).*

6-Card Reading: Jane

Relationships
*Jane wanted to resolve
a relationship dilemma and
was seeking guidance.*

Card one—the Hermit

The Hermit indicated that Jane needed time to reflect on her somewhat traumatic relationship pattern, as well as looking at where she stood in the present relationship. This was particularly testing for Jane—she admitted that even if a relationship was bad, she preferred being with someone to being alone. The Hermit suggested that she could discover much about herself and the answers to the questions she was seeking if she was patient and dared to spend some time on her own.

Card two—the Tower

The Tower stressed the fact that it was time for Jane to reassess her values and her relationships with others. She was beginning to recognize that her attraction to unsuitable men was based on a fear of intimacy. This kept her in inhibiting relationships that prevented her from expressing who she was. Only a major reevaluation of herself could change this dynamic.

Card three—Strength

Strength in the position of Helpful Influences suggested that no matter how challenging it was for Jane to confront herself and change some fundamental aspects of her life, she had the determination to do so. Initiating these changes would enhance her sense of self-worth and help her to integrate the more positive aspects of her nature.

Card four—the Lovers

The Lovers card confirmed the fact that Jane was facing a choice in the area of relationships. Her existing relationship

would be tested as she began to
question her motives for being with her
partner, and she now had the potential
to discover what it was that she most
valued and could therefore live in
accordance with her true self.

Card five—the Hierophant

The Hierophant appeared in the place
of the Unconscious, indicating that it
was time for Jane to find a more
meaningful and possibly spiritual
context to her life. As a result of the
crisis she was going through, she might
meet someone who could guide her to
a deeper understanding of herself.

Card six—Temperance

This was a hopeful card for Jane to pick
and suggested that provided she took
the time to explore and reevaluate her
feelings, there was every chance that
she would find a happy and
harmonious relationship. Rather than
always being the one doing the giving,
she could achieve greater balance and
a more equal kind of partnership.

THE NINE-CARD SPREAD
The nine-card spread covers the past, present, and future and is especially helpful in uncovering what is at the root of a particular problem. This spread was used for Rick, aged 25, who consulted the cards about problems with his health. He had been suffering from chronic headaches and fatigue, but tests had found that there was no medical explanation for his condition. His previous relationship had ended traumatically because he was unable to make a commitment. Rick was hoping that the cards would reveal the deeper, underlying reason for his "disease."

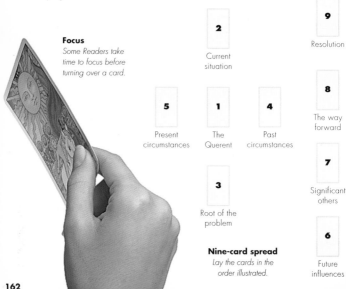

Focus
Some Readers take time to focus before turning over a card.

9
Resolution

2
Current situation

5
Present circumstances

1
The Querent

4
Past circumstances

8
The way forward

3
Root of the problem

7
Significant others

6
Future influences

Nine-card spread
Lay the cards in the order illustrated.

THREE OF SWORDS

NINE OF CUPS

SIX OF CUPS

DEATH

EIGHT OF CUPS

NINE OF WANDS

QUEEN OF WANDS

FIVE OF CUPS

PAGE OF CUPS

Case study
*This nine-card spread was drawn
by Rick (see page 164).*

9-Card Reading: Rick

Troubles
*Health concerns and the end
of a relationship prompted Rick
to consult the cards.*

Card one—Death

This card suggested that Rick needed to let go of his present way of life. A complete change was required so that he could free himself of whatever was burdening him and start anew.

Card two—Three of Swords

This card suggested that he may not have come to terms with the breakup of his relationship and the negative effect that it was having on his life and health. It was important that he became aware of how unhappy he was.

Card three—Five of Cups

The Five of Cups highlighted Rick's disappointment and regret over his choice to break up with his girlfriend. This had obviously weighed heavily on him and caused him to feel quite a lot of despair about his ability to sustain a long-term relationship. This card suggested that all was not lost and there was still something left to work on.

Card four—Eight of Cups

The depression that Rick had experienced and the pain that he had suffered from the loss of his last relationship was patently obvious from the appearance of this card.

Card five—Six of Cups

This card very succinctly described the nostalgia Rick felt about happier times spent in the past with his girlfriend. It also suggested that his former love might reappear in his life and if so, they would have the chance to rebuild a life together based on the lessons learned from what had gone on in the past.

Card six—Page of Cups

The message of this card is emotional renewal: after a period of hurt and withdrawal, Rick needed to forgive himself and stop punishing himself for the mistakes of the past, and his heart would open to love.

Card seven—Queen of Wands

The woman that Rick was still in love with appeared here as warm, loving, loyal, and sympathetic. If he confided in her about his feelings, he had a good chance of winning her back.

Card eight—Nine of Wands

A setback or delay in the pursuit of Rick's goal wouldn't dampen his determination. He knew what he wanted and any obstacles along the way would only strengthen his resolve.

Card nine—Nine of Cups

A happy outcome. It looked as if Rick would be ready to make an emotional commitment and finally enjoy true happiness and contentment.

THE NINE-CARD SPREAD: 2

This spread was used when Sally, aged 25, came for a reading. Sally worked as a financial consultant. Her job was extremely high-powered and she worked very long hours. She had reached a crossroads in her life and was debating whether to accept a promotion that would entail more responsibility and even longer hours, or to have a baby. Her husband was particularly keen to start a family. Sally had conflicting emotions.

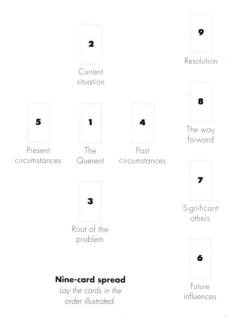

2

Current situation

9

Resolution

5

Present circumstances

1

The Querent

4

Past circumstances

8

The way forward

3

Root of the problem

7

Significant others

6

Future influences

Nine-card spread
Lay the cards in the order illustrated.

THREE OF CUPS

TWO OF SWORDS

SIX OF SWORDS

SEVEN OF
PENTACLES

THE EMPRESS

SEVEN OF
SWORDS

KNIGHT OF SWORDS

THE CHARIOT

Case study

*This nine-card spread was
drawn by Sally (see page 168).*

QUEEN OF CUPS

9-Card Reading: Sally

Dilemma

*Sally needed to make
a major life decision:
family or career?*

Card one—the Empress

Although Sally did not yet see herself as a mother, this card strongly indicated the possibility of getting pregnant and giving birth. She was feeling a strong need for emotional harmony and well-being and was entering a cycle where the need to nurture her body was of prime importance.

Card two—Two of Swords

This card reflected stalemate: Sally was unable to reach a decision and this had led to conflict with her husband.

Card three—the Chariot

This depicted Sally's struggle: deciding between career and baby was pulling her apart and creating a huge amount of inner tension.

Card four—Seven of Swords

This reflected the uncomfortable feeling that Sally had from not dealing directly with her ambivalent feelings and discussing them with her husband.

Card five—Seven of Pentacles

A clear perspective on Sally's situation. She needed to think very carefully about whether to opt for a promotion or put her energies into becoming a mother.

Card six—Queen of Cups

Sally would be getting more in touch with her intuition with the appearance of this card. Becoming more in tune with her feelings would also increase her sensitivity to those around her. Not only would this help her to make the right choice, but it would make her more sympathetic to her husband.

Card seven—Knight of Swords

The Knight of Swords represented a strong ally of Sally's who would be able to help her resolve her current conflict. Whether this was a colleague, sibling, or friend, he or she would have the power to motivate her to try something unknown and different. This could also suggest that Sally needed to handle her situation and not procrastinate if she wanted to be effective.

Card eight—Six of Swords

This was an encouraging card for Sally and indicated that she would soon move away from the stressful situation she was in and resolve her dilemma. The future looked bright and she could look forward to a less anxious time.

Card nine—Three of Cups

An emotionally fulfilling time lay ahead and Sally would soon be able to put the past behind her. A new creative phase was starting and a joyful celebration, perhaps the birth of a child, was certainly on the cards.

READING THE SUITS

The four suits of the Minor Arcana represent the four elements; fire, air, earth, and water. When there is an emphasis of any suit in a spread, it means that the qualities that suit represents are of prime importance to the reading. Although the meaning of the Major Arcana carries more weight than that of the Minor Arcana, the suits do offer greater clarity and depth to the picture.

WANDS

CUPS

Eight of Cups
Giving up and walking away from a painful situation is indicated.

Eight of Wands
Movement after a period of delay is the message of the Eight of Wands.

Elements
Tarot readers understand the suits in terms of their natural elements.

SWORDS

PENTACLES

Eight of Pentacles

A new job opportunity is signified by the Eight of Pentacles.

Eight of Swords

This describes a situation that is difficult to deal with.

The Four Elements

The four elements
These are fire, air, water, and earth. Each represents certain qualities and affinities.

The four elements are found in many esoteric traditions, such as medieval alchemy and shamanism. They are interconnected and all serve to sustain life. When they are not in balance, however, they can have a negative effect and an excess of any one element can be destructive. The elements are also reminiscent of the seasons, and as you familiarize yourself with the Tarot the natural images of the elements will become familiar motifs. In medieval times, artists equated the ancient astrological symbols of the lion, the bull, the eagle, and the angel with the four cardinal elements and with the four seasons. These were later associated with the Hebrew word *Jehovah*, which was understood to be the consciously directed energy from which the entire universe was created.

Domination

If Wands dominate there will be an opportunity for new growth in the area of career, and if Cups figure strongly there will be an emphasis on emotional matters. A preponderance of Pentacles will place more importance on the five senses and the material world, and lots of Swords will denote mental conflict or a spiritual struggle, and standing strong in adversity. In the Minor Arcana, the Court cards, like the Pip cards, are in suits, and the elements associated with the suits influences the personalities of the characters depicted.

The zodiac

In astrology, the twelve signs of the zodiac are divided into the four elements and there are some Tarot decks that incorporate astrological symbolism in their design. The four-fold division of the elements also has a correlation with Jung's four types: feeling is associated with fire, sensation is linked to earth, thinking is associated with air, and intuition correlates with water.

One way to understand the journey of the Suits from ace to king is to see them as a creative process that begins with the spark of inspiration (the element of fire). The element of Water then absorbs the initial impulse to realize something, and our imagination can then dream up various ways in which we can give birth to that idea. The mental element of air then plans and develops the concept further until earth, the element of concrete actualization, manifests the final stage of the project.

Elementary

Each suit of the Minor Arcana is associated with an element. This influences the personalities and characteristics that are depicted on the Court Cards.

THE JUNGIAN SPREAD
Animus, the masculine principle in Jungian psychology, means wind, breath, or spirit. Anima, the feminine, means soul. In the following spread, the animus represents the father-figure within us that tells us what we should do and how we should be, regardless of whether that is how our true self wishes to behave. The anima card represents the mother-figure in all of us who serves as a reminder of what we need to do for others and ourselves. The other card in this spread is the child, and reveals who we really are and how we would most authentically express ourselves if there were no inhibiting factors. When the pack is shuffled and cut, take one card to represent the Significator and three others to represent the animus, anima, and the child.

Carl Jung
In Jungian psychology every man and woman carries an inner image of their opposite gender, which often embodies all that they seek in the other. These images are unconscious and often projected onto those whose qualities match the inner image we carry. Jung described these unconscious images as animus and anima. Jung spent much of his life studying mythology, alchemy, and symbolism.

THE FOOL   KNIGHT OF WANDS   THE MOON   PAGE OF WANDS

Case study

This Jungian spread was drawn by Anita (see page 176).

 1

2

3

 4

The   Animus   Anima   Child
Significator

The Jungian spread

Lay the cards in the order illustrated.

First move

Shuffle and cut the cards in the usual way before laying them out.

Jungian Reading: Anita

Pastures new
A completely new life, involving moving to another country, was a probability for Anita.

Anita, aged 26, had been in a steady but rather boring job for a couple of years. She had recently been to Madagascar on vacation and had fallen in love with both the country and somebody she had met there. On her return, life felt lackluster and she longed to return to the place that had captured her heart.

Card one—the Fool

This card was particularly apt since it indicated that Anita was ready to make a fresh start in her life. It also reflected the fact that a risk was involved in this new venture, because Anita was going into the unknown. She was uncertain about how she could make a living in Madagascar, but she was ready to break out of her mold and the Fool indicated that new horizons were opening up for her. However, she needed to avoid the temptation of rushing headlong into a new situation without first assessing the pros and cons. It was possible that her naivety was clouding her judgement.

Card two—Knight of Wands

The Knight of Wands suggested that Anita was identified with the fiery masculine energy of this card. The man she had fallen in love with also fitted this particular image and her attraction to him reflected the fact that those same qualities were emerging in her own psyche. She was full of enthusiasm and excitement at the prospect of doing something adventurous, particularly since she felt that she had never fully expressed this side of her nature before.

Card three—the Moon

Anita was in the grip of some powerful, unconscious feelings, which were making it hard for her to come to an objective decision. Her fantasy about starting a new life was all-consuming and it was very difficult for her to separate fact from fiction. She felt compelled to go abroad and yet felt anxious about leaving her everyday life and safe, predictable world behind. The Moon suggested that she could be deceiving herself about what her new life held in store. Only time would tell whether her dreams had any basis in reality, and whether she would find happiness abroad.

Card four—Page of Wands

This card consolidated the theme of the reading. Anita needed to express her adventurous and fun-loving side and take up the exciting opportunity of a new life. Although her decision might seem rash and impulsive to others, she truly felt inspired to embark on this quest and follow her heart's desire.

Crossroads
The Options spread is perfect if you are unsure which direction to take in life.

THE OPTIONS SPREAD: 1

This is a good spread for those who are at some sort of crossroads in life, such as John, aged 65, a lecturer approaching retirement. Although he looked forward to devoting more time to his numerous hobbies, he was also attracted to another very tempting prospect. A publishing company had asked him to write a book and much of the research would involve a fair amount of travel. He hoped that the cards would clarify his options.

| 1 | INITIAL CARD | 1 |

| 2 | | 2 |

| 3 | | 3 |

| FIRST OPTION | | SECOND OPTION |

Reading the future
The Options reading describes two different choices and their likely outcome.

FOUR OF
PENTACLES

EIGHT OF
PENTACLES

ACE OF SWORDS

KNIGHT OF
PENTACLES

Case study

*This Options spread
was drawn by John
(see page 180).
After placing the initial
card, the cards down the
left and right represent
his two choices.*

EIGHT OF WANDS

THE HERMIT

THE WORLD

Options Reading: John

New horizons
There was an exciting challenge in prospect for John as he approached retirement.

Initial card—Eight of Pentacles

The Eight of Pentacles signified that John would feel a great sense of satisfaction from putting his talents and abilities to good use. This would either be through enjoyment of his hobbies or from exploiting his talent as a writer. The latter offered the opportunity for an emotionally rewarding, as well as lucrative, new profession with no age bar. John was ready to develop more of his potential and by putting his abilities to work, he would gain a new lease of life.

Option 1—retirement

Card one—Four of Pentacles

This warned John against holding too tightly onto what he already had because this would block his chance to grow and move forward. John intended to live very frugally if he retired since he was concerned about his financial security. This threatened to undermine his sense of well-being.

Card two—Knight of Pentacles

This card illustrates the steady pace of life that John would adopt if he went into retirement. Life would not be challenging or exciting, but there would be a reassuring predictability and calm.

Card three—the Hermit

A quiet contemplative existence was the message of this card and it indicated that John would spend plenty of time alone in his retirement. The pace of his life would slow down considerably and he would reconcile himself to growing older and to his own mortality.

Option 2—writing/traveling

Card one—Ace of Swords

This suggested inevitable change. If John took up the book offer, he would connect with a powerful new mental energy to help him meet the challenge. The great power of this card showed that there was much to achieve if John chose this route.

Card two—Eight of Wands

A very exciting and inspiring period in John's life. Everything looked set to go smoothly and John's career would take off in ways that he couldn't previously have imagined.

Card three—the World

Worldly success and a deep sense of achievement. He would gain much by taking this path and be richly rewarded for his efforts. He would be able to integrate every aspect of himself in this project and attain a sense of resolution and completion to his life's work. Many opportunities would present themselves.

THE OPTIONS SPREAD: 2

Jackie, aged 21, had been going out with her boyfriend Alan since she was 18. She had assumed that they would eventually get married. However, a few weeks prior to coming for a reading, she had met David. He was a few years older than her, had been married, and was recently divorced. The attraction between them was immediate and threw Jackie into instant confusion. She did not know whether to continue with her boyfriend or to end the relationship so that she could begin seeing David.

1	INITIAL CARD	1
2		2
3		3
FIRST OPTION		SECOND OPTION

Strong-willed
Power, strength and stability are all represented by The Emperor.

182

TWO OF SWORDS

THE HIEROPHANT

NINE OF SWORDS

THE HIEROPHANT

Case study

This Options spread was drawn by Jackie (see page 184). On the left is the option to continue the relationship. On the right is the option to start a new relationship.

SEVEN OF CUPS

THE DEVIL

SEVEN OF CUPS

TEN OF WANDS

THE STAR

Options Reading: Jackie

Two men

Jackie came for guidance on a dilemma. Had she outgrown her relationship with Alan?

Initial card—Two of Swords

This card aptly describes the impasse that Jackie was in. She knew how hurt and upset Alan would be if she ended their relationship. She faced a difficult choice, but honesty was her best policy.

Option 1—continue her relationship with Alan

Card one—Nine of Swords

The Nine of Swords describes the guilt and sense of foreboding that Jackie had about ending her relationship with Alan.

Her sense of trepidation about his reaction was creating a great deal of anxiety and fear. It was important for Jackie to be aware of how many negative feelings she was projecting on the situation and try to get a truer perspective on her doubts and fears. She may have been carrying a burden of guilt from a past breakup, either her own or perhaps that of her parents.

Card two—the Devil

This card signifies a feeling of being trapped. Jackie felt ashamed of herself for being attracted to another man and was struggling to come to terms with her conflicting emotions. While Jackie was held captive by these powerful feelings, she would be unable to resolve her dilemma.

Card three—Ten of Wands

This describes how weighed down Jackie felt, which made her exhausted as a result. Her way of thinking was holding her back and preventing her from moving on in her life.

Option 2—start a new relationship with David

Card one—the Hierophant

This symbolized David's presence in Jackie's life, and suggested that his role would be that of a mentor or wise teacher, and that Jackie was ready to grow in maturity and self-awareness.

Card two—Seven of Cups

This underscored the fact that Jackie had a choice in love. It showed much potential for happiness and fulfillment in a future relationship with David, but she would need to be fully aware of the implications of her choice, as well as adopting a realistic and practical approach to the new relationship.

Card three—the Star

The Star concludes the very positive influence that was indicated by this option. Jackie could confidently expect a bright future once she had freed herself of any remorse or guilt. A new life with David looked very promising.

THE SEVEN-CARD HORSESHOE

This spread gives guidance on a specific problem. After the cards have been shuffled and cut, lay them out in a semicircle from left to right, card one on the left and card seven on the right. Card one reflects the past and its influence, card two the present, card three the future, card four the best course of action, card five significant others, card six obstacles, and card seven the outcome. The cards can be read as a whole and not necessarily in order.

Lucky or not?
Difficult issues can be clarified with the Horseshoe Spread.

1 *Shuffle and cut the cards before laying them out.*

2 Lay the cards in a semicircle from left to right.

3 Turn the cards up starting from the left.

First card

Horseshoe Answers

Preparation
*Laying out the cards in
a semicircle in preparation
for the reading.*

The Tarot rarely gives a definite yes
or no answer, but it can give a
fairly strong indication of how to
deal with a situation. The Seven-card
Horseshoe is a good spread for giving
guidance when the Querent is unsure
of what to do about a problem.

After the cards have been shuffled
and selected, the chosen cards are laid
out according to the pattern in the
picture. The first card reveals a specific
aspect of the past that will relate to the
current problem about which the Querent
is seeking advice. It might describe
events that have led up to the present
situation, or it could allude to a similar
past situation and remind the Querent of
how he dealt with it. Even if there is no
obvious connection between the past
situation and the present problem, this
card will indicate how best to draw on
his past experience.

Card two reflects the present and
highlights whatever the Querent is
concerned about. Look at this card in
relation to cards one (the past) and
three (the future) to deduce whether
circumstances will get better or worse.

Card number three represents the
immediate future and card number four
indicates the best course of action to
resolve the issue. To see whether the
Querent will in fact follow that route or
decide on another direction can be
assessed by looking at this card in
relation to cards three and seven. This
should shed further light on what is
influencing the Querent's decision.

Cards five to seven

The card in position five indicates
whether those around the Querent are
behaving in a supportive or unhelpful
way. The card in position six reveals
any obstacles to resolving the problem.
The Querent may be aware of these
problems or this card could be alerting
him to an obstacle that he has not
anticipated. If this is a favorable card, it
is more difficult to interpret and you will
need to see how the meaning of the
card could in some way pose a
problem for the Querent.

Card number seven may sum up the
Querent's attitude to the whole situation,
or describe the course of action that he
is most likely to take. Although the
number of each card indicates the order
in which they are to be laid out, you
can be somewhat flexible in the order
in which you interpret them. Find a way
of reading the cards that feels most
appropriate and meaningful to you,
and assess the relationship between the
cards in whichever way you find most
constructive and revealing.

THE ASTROLOGICAL SPREAD

The Astrological spread is very useful for looking at the different areas of someone's life. The meaning of the twelve categories is very similar to the twelve houses of the astrological horoscope. You can read this spread in two ways, either as a way of gaining an overview of the present circumstances, or as a guide for the year ahead, with the first card signifying the current month, the second card the following month. You can use just the 22 cards of the Major Arcana or the whole deck. After the cards have been shuffled and cut, lay them out counterclockwise in a circle. This spread was ideal for Jo, aged 35, a freelance journalist. Jo wanted a greater understanding of the patterns at work in her life.

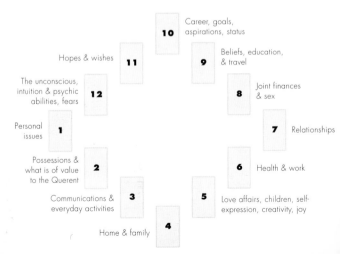

10 Career, goals, aspirations, status

11 Hopes & wishes

9 Beliefs, education, & travel

12 The unconscious, intuition & psychic abilities, fears

8 Joint finances & sex

1 Personal issues

7 Relationships

2 Possessions & what is of value to the Querent

6 Health & work

3 Communications & everyday activities

5 Love affairs, children, self-expression, creativity, joy

4 Home & family

SEVEN OF
WANDS

THE SUN

THE
HIEROPHANT

SIX OF
PENTACLES

THE
HANGED MAN

DEATH

Case study

*This Astrological spread
was drawn by Jo (see
page 192).*

QUEEN OF
WANDS

TWO OF
PENTACLES

TEN OF
WANDS

ACE OF
WANDS

THREE OF
SWORDS

KNIGHT
OF CUPS

Astrological Reading: Jo

Journalist

Jo had recently got a well-paid new job. She wanted to take a deeper look at herself.

Card one—Queen of Wands

The Queen of Wands reflected Jo's warm, outgoing, sociable personality. She was very popular.

Card two—Two of Pentacles

This card suggested that she had the resources, both emotionally and financially, to make a success of life.

Card three—Ace of Wands

This highlighted her creative abilities, and the new job now put her in a position to develop her talents.

Card four—Three of Swords

Jo's ten-year marriage had been shaky for a while and a separation now seemed inevitable. She hoped that this would clear the way for a new start.

Card five—Knight of Cups

The spirit of romance was about to enter her life—a surprise to Jo as she had not expected to fall in love.

Card six—Ten of Wands

The message of the card here was that Jo needed to address the issues that were wearing her down emotionally. This would release her energy so that she was in a better position to embrace the new creative phase that was just beginning in her life.

Card seven—Death

Clearly this card was heralding the end of one cycle of Jo's life and the beginning of another. It indicated the final ending of her marriage, and also promised the opportunity of a new life if she was willing to let go of the past.

Card eight—Six of Pentacles

This suggested that Jo would benefit from someone's generosity and her trust in life would be renewed.

Card nine—the Hierophant

This represented her spiritual and intellectual aspirations and developing need to explore new beliefs and ideas.

Card ten—Seven of Wands

Stiff competition at work was indicated here informing Jo that she needed to draw on all of her skills and abilities in order to prove herself.

Card eleven—the Sun

There would be every opportunity to realize her ambitions. She would also enjoy much happiness in all of her personal relationships.

Card twelve—the Hanged Man

Unresolved fears would be brought to light. She had reached a turning point and needed to trust that something of greater value would come into her life.

THE GOLDEN DAWN

This spread is named after one that was used by the Order of the Golden Dawn. It is a very comprehensive spread and gives an in-depth picture of the Querent's situation. It also describes the various options that lie before the Querent, as well as the best course of action to follow. This spread does not give a likely outcome but rather focuses on the fact that the Querent makes his own choice.

Golden Dawn
The Order of the Golden Dawn was of crucial importance to the development of the Tarot (see page 20).

Sephiroth
The Tree of Life is a symbolic way of understanding the relationship between the ten Sephiroth.

Winged
The Devil from the New Golden Dawn Tarot.

Heavenly
The Prince of Swords from the New Golden Dawn Tarot.

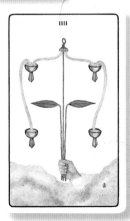

Flowing
The Four of Cups from the New Golden Dawn Tarot.

Fiery
The King of Wands from the New Golden Dawn Tarot.

Golden Dawn Spread

There are three cards for each position and these need to be interpreted in relation to one another. Cards one, two, and three describe the Querent, one shows her personality or feelings at this time and the other two either elaborate on this or reveal something about the present situation. Cards four, eight, and twelve indicate what will most likely transpire if the Querent continues with the course of action that she is motivated to take at this moment. Each card will either show a sequence of events or a different aspect of what is likely to happen. You will need to decide which is the most appropriate interpretation.

Make a decision

Cards five, nine, and thirteen represent alternative courses of action if the Querent decides against going with

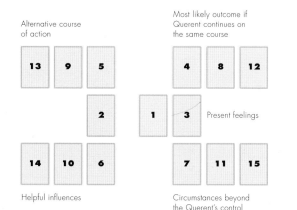

Alternative course
of action

Most likely outcome if
Querent continues on
the same course

Present feelings

Helpful influences

Circumstances beyond
the Querent's control

four, eight, and twelve. Compare and contrast these two sets of cards to see which is the better alternative.

Cards six, ten, and fourteen indicate what can help the Querent to make a decision. This could be helpful people or aspects of the situation, which need to be carefully considered before reaching a final decision. Compare these cards with what has already been discussed to see whether they are underlining a previous point or revealing something new.

Cards seven, eleven, and fifteen show the circumstances that are beyond the Querent's control, but still need to be considered when deciding what to do. Even though these circumstances cannot be changed, there are still choices in terms of how the Querent deals with them.

Positioning

In the Golden Dawn spread there are three cards for each position and each card needs to be interpreted in relation to the other two cards.

GOLDEN DAWN READING
Alex, aged 21, had just graduated from university when she came for a reading. She had obtained a first-class degree and had been offered a very good job, but yearned to travel for a year before starting work.

THREE OF WANDS

KING OF WANDS

STRENGTH

Making a decision
Alex wanted to look at her options in greater detail, so the Golden Dawn spread was the ideal one to use to help her choose the best course of action.

THE TOWER

JUSTICE

WHEEL OF FORTUNE

NINE OF WANDS

FIVE OF PENTACLES

TWO OF SWORDS

THE DEVIL

FOUR OF CUPS

KNIGHT OF SWORDS

THE MOON

FIVE OF WANDS

EIGHT OF SWORDS

Golden Dawn Reading: Alex

Card one—Four of Cups
Alex felt dissatisfied and restless.

Card two—the Tower
The Tower indicated Alex's upheaval and turmoil.

Card three—Knight of Swords
Although Alex was confused there were new opportunites on the horizon.

Card four—Five of Pentacles
If she chose to go straight to work she may have felt she'd compromised.

Card five—Strength
Alex would have the courage of her convictions. This would be uplifting.

Card six—Nine of Wands
Alex would overcome any obstacles.

Card seven—the Moon
She felt excited and determined, but there were underlying fears.

Graduate
Alex hoped the cards would shed some light on her desire for greater freedom.

Card eight—Two of Swords
Alex would feel trapped in her job.

Card nine—King of Wands
The idea of going away was exciting —she was ready for the challenge.

Card ten—Wheel of Fortune
Unexpected changes were in store.

Card eleven—Five of Wands
She needed to hold on to her vision to travel, but needed to remain realistic.

Card twelve—the Devil

The message of the Two of Swords was reinforced here and suggested that Alex would feel angry and frustrated by the circumstances at work.

Card thirteen—Three of Wands

Alex was excited and optimistic about the thought of an adventure. She had the courage to explore new territory.

Card fourteen—Justice

Alex needed to consider her options carefully. It was important to maintain the courage of her convictions and adopt a rational, balanced perspective.

Card fifteen—Eight of Swords

Alex longed to break free but fear that she might make a wrong decision and jeopardize her future held her back. She needed to confront those who opposed her but, more importantly, the aspects of herself that undermined her. She could then make her decision.

Ancient symbol
The Celtic cross, the symbol and inspiration for this Tarot spread.

THE CELTIC CROSS: 1

The Celtic Cross is one of the best known and most popular spreads of the Tarot because it gives an excellent overview of the Querent's situation. It can be used with the whole pack or only the 22 cards of the Major Arcana. This layout is very good for general situations, as well as for answering a specific question.

Youthful
The Knight is often used to signify a young adult of either gender.

Courtly
Traditionally a Court card is used in the Celtic Cross to represent the Significator.

Significator
When determining which suit to use for the Significator, you can either use the element that belongs to their Sun sign, or base the choice on their character.

The Queen is often chosen as the Significator if a woman consults the cards.

Celtic Cross Spread

Ever since Arthur Waite featured the Celtic Cross in the Pictorial Key to the Tarot, almost every Tarot book has included a version of it. Its immense popularity among Tarot readers is perhaps due to the fact that it works on many different levels and is open to a variety of interpretations. As well as addressing the Querent's hopes and fears, it also gives an insight into aspects of the Querent's nature and circumstances that they may not be fully aware of. These insights can help the Querent to understand the part they themselves play in shaping their own situation and destiny. The predictive element of the spread indicates what is likely to happen, but as we already know, the cards cannot and do not predict a fixed or fated future. Our future is shaped by how we live our day to day lives.

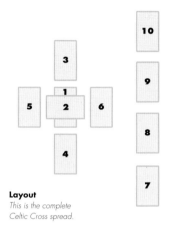

Layout
This is the complete Celtic Cross spread.

Circle and cross

The Celtic Cross is made up of two parts, which resemble the two parts of the standing cross that is so well-known in Ireland. The standing cross incorporates a circle and a cross together upon an upright.

Laying out the cards

After the cards have been shuffled and cut, lay them out in the following order. Place card number one down (the Querent's present position) and then lay card number two (immediate influences) across it. Card number three (what is most apparent in the Querent's life) should be placed above cards one and two, and card number four (what is at the root of the reading) goes beneath them. Lay the fifth card (past influences) to the left of cards one and two and the sixth card (future influences) to the right. You have now formed the cross.

Build a vertical line to the right of the cross with the four remaining cards, starting at the bottom with the seventh card (the Querent's feeling), number eight (outside influences), number nine (hopes and fears), and number ten (the outcome).

Some packs include a cloth, usually black in color, for the protection of the cards, with the designated layout of the cards already printed onto the material. This makes the process of laying out the spread very straightforward, as well as giving a strong background to the laid-out cards.

Make Some Space

If you are sitting at a table to do your reading, make sure that you have plenty of space so that you are able to spread out the cards in the correct order.

Cross purposes
*The Ace of Swords
from the New Golden
Dawn Tarot.*

THE CELTIC CROSS: 2

Two cards are laid at a central point, the second card crosses the first representing immediate influences. A cross is then formed by laying cards 3, 4, 5, and 6. A second vertical cross is then built which represents the upright cross. It is laid to the right and contains four cards.

Card one
*The Sun indicates the Querent's
present position.*

Card two
*The Nine of Wands represents
immediate influences.*

Stage one

The cross formed by cards one and two, and the circle formed by cards three, four, five, and six, represent the first stage of the Celtic Cross.

NINE OF PENTACLES

TEN OF PENTACLES

NINE OF SWORDS

EIGHT OF CUPS

TEN OF CUPS

FIVE OF WANDS

FOUR OF CUPS

TWO OF PENTACLES

Celtic Cross: A Spread

Sunlight
The Sun is one of the most auspicious cards in the Tarot and denotes joy and fulfillment.

Card one—The Sun

This denotes a time of healing, well-being, self-confidence, and enthusiasm for life. It expresses hope, optimism, creativity, individuality, insight, and a sense of purpose.

Card two—The Nine of Wands

Indicates an obstacle that needs to be surmounted before the final goal is reached. Determination and faith in his intuition will equip the Querent to achieve whatever he has set out to do.

Card three—Ten of Pentacles

Describes a happy life with a feeling of emotional and material security. This card epitomizes the contentment that comes from a happy family life.

Card four—Four of Cups

Indicates that the Querent has needed a period of solitude to recharge his batteries after illness or work stress.

Card five—Eight of Cups

Describes an emotional upheaval in the Querent's life, which may have left him feeling downhearted and disillusioned, but no positive changes can take place until the past has been relinquished.

Card six—Ten of Cups

Promises the realization of a heartfelt wish, and a joyful event such as a wedding or the birth of a child.

Card seven—Two of Pentacles

Suggests that the Querent has the ability, emotional and physical stamina to make a success of anything.

Card eight—Five of Wands

Describes competition with others and putting one's skills to the test. There are obstacles to overcome and the Querent will need to be patient and believe that he can succeed.

Card nine—Nine of Swords

Suggests that deep-seated fears and anxieties are creating a strong sense of foreboding. Uncovering the root of these fears will be liberating.

Card ten—Nine of Pentacles

The outcome of the reading is extremely positive and suggests that the Querent will have a sense of pride and accomplishment in what he has been able to achieve. He has worked hard to acquire a sense of self-worth and it is not dependent on anyone or anything.

Specific Questions

Unlike other Tarot spreads, the Celtic Cross can answer specific questions as well as giving the Querent a general overview of a particular situation.

THE CELTIC CROSS: 3

All of the cards are now laid out in the Celtic Cross spread and are ready to be interpreted. Although each card holds a specific position and will be interpreted according to the meaning of that position, it is important to synthesize all of the cards into a meaningful whole.

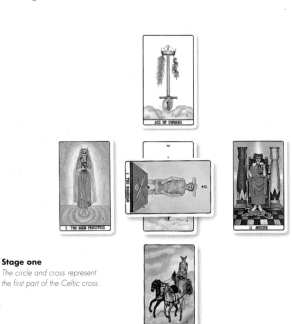

Stage one
The circle and cross represent the first part of the Celtic cross.

The World

In position ten this card denotes great achievement.

The Emperor

In position nine the Emperor signifies self-worth and success.

Strength

In position eight this card represents self-confidence and the will to succeed.

Hierophant

The Hierophant in position seven symbolizes a spiritual teacher or mentor.

Imperious
The Emperor signifies worldly power.

Case Study: Kate

New job problems
A crisis in confidence over the demands of her new job motivated Kate to have a reading.

Soon after graduating, aged 21, Kate had found her dream job. After a couple of months, she was having serious doubts about whether she was up to it. The reading was particularly significant; it contained no less than seven Major Arcana cards.

Card one—Seven of Pentacles

This card affirmed Kate's achievements and also underlined the current setback. She had the power to make a success of her situation if she could believe in herself and work on her self-esteem.

Card two—the Magician

This suggested that she was not yet fully aware of how gifted and talented she really was. She needed to make a positive decision to develop her confidence and potential.

Card three—Ace of Swords

This heralded that Kate would be able to get a clear perspective on what was blocking her from believing in herself and take steps to overcome it. A shift in attitude was about to take place.

Card four—the Chariot

This described Kate's crisis of confidence when she was offered the job and had been in two minds as to whether to accept it.

Card five—the High Priestess

Justice described the decision that Kate had been required to make in respect of her job offer. She had weighed up the pros and cons and come to a balanced decision without being swayed by her conflicting emotions.

Card six—Justice

The opportunity to become more in touch with her intuition would help her understand herself better.

Card seven—the Hierophant

This reflected the fact that Kate felt the need to turn to someone who could guide and support her.

Card eight—Strength

Kate's peers and colleagues recognized her strengths and acknowledged how talented and gifted she was.

Card Nine—the Emperor

This card indicated that once she was able to let go of her self-doubt, she could achieve great things in the world.

Card ten—the World

The outcome of the reading pointed to everything that Kate would be able to achieve. She would gain much self-knowledge and self-confidence, begin to accept herself wholeheartedly, and be proud of her achievements.

PERSONAL DEVELOPMENT

The many themes, images, and symbols of the Tarot lend themselves beautifully to meditation and discovering more about yourself. Visualized meditations tap into the unconscious mind and create spontaneous mental images. The response that we have to these images can be revealing and may bring to light hidden aspects of our personalities. When we connect with this new awareness, it can act as a spur for our future growth and development and give us a deeper and more meaningful sense of who we are and what is trying to unfold in our lives at any given moment.

The Star
Signifies hope and faith in a better and brighter future.

Ten of Cups
Symbolizes happiness, contentment, and the realization of a heartfelt desire.

It is a good idea to keep a Tarot journal to record your insights, feelings, and understanding of the cards and the spreads as a whole. Keeping a journal helps to develop a deeper awareness of yourself through your growing relationship with the cards.

Visualization

Visualizing the cards in meditation will help you to create a dynamic relationship with the imagery and symbolism.

Creates spontaneous mental images

Brings cards to life

Nine of Wands

Represents the courage and determination to overcome any obstacles.

GLOSSARY

Alchemy The ancient science that attempted to turn base metals into gold. On another level this was understood as a quest for personal transformation.

Aleister Crowley A member of the Hermetic Order of the Golden Dawn. He left in 1905 and formed his own order, Argenteum Astrum. Crowley was a notorious devotee of the occult and went on to publish the *Book of Thoth*, along with Lady Frieda Harris, in 1944.

Anima The unconscious inner image of the feminine that a man carries. Anima means soul.

Animus The unconscious inner image of the masculine that a woman carries. Animus means breath, wind, or spirit.

Arcana From the Latin word *arcanum*, meaning secret or mystery.

Archetypal A pattern that is universal and exists in all people, and in all cultures and periods of history.

Book of Thoth Name of the Tarot pack designed by Aleister Crowley.

Cabbala Jewish mystical teachings from which, it is believed, the Tarot originates.

Carl Jung A Swiss psychologist who came up with the principle of synchronicity, which propounds that everything in the world is connected.

Cartomancy Using cards for divination.

Celtic Cross The most popular spread that reflects life on both an archetypal and ordinary level.

Court cards The Page, the Knight, the King, and the Queen cards.

Cups One of the four suits of the Minor Arcana associated with the element of Water, and related to love, feelings, and dreams.

Divination A method of acquiring knowledge that is not available by ordinary means.

Dualism The idea that the universe is comprised of opposites. Some people believe that the aim of the Tarot is to resolve these apparent conflicts.

Esoteric Hidden, spiritual teachings.

Elements Fundamental qualities of existence. In Tarot and astrology these are: Fire, Water, Air, and Earth.

Hermetic Order of the Golden Dawn Late 19th-century esoteric society that believed astrology, alchemy, divination, numerology, and the cabbala all belonged to one esoteric system to which the Tarot was the central key.

I Ching A Chinese book and method of divination.

Major Arcana The 22 cards that represent major life events and spiritual issues.

Minor Arcana The four suits of the Tarot. Each suit contains cards numbered from ace (zero) to ten, as well as the Page, Knight, Queen, and King.

Meditation A way of stilling the mind and calming the body in order to heighten spiritual awareness.

Numerology The study of numbers and how they relate to our lives. Numerology is linked closely with Tarot and astrology.

Pentacles (also called Disks or Coins). A suit of the Minor Arcana associated with the element of earth, and related to material and financial matters.

Pip cards The numbered cards of the Major Arcana.

Querent The person seeking a Tarot reading.

Reader The person who lays out the Tarot cards and interprets them.

Reversed cards An optional way of reading the cards in an upside-down position. This changes the meaning of the card and gives each card more scope for interpretation.

Rider-Waite Pack The best known Tarot pack, designed by Arthur Edward Waite and Pamela Colman Smith.

Runes Ancient Norse method of divination.

Sephiroth The ten circles of divine energy that form the Tree of Life.

Significator A card chosen by the Tarot reader to represent the Querent.

Spread The different ways in which the cards are laid out for a reading.

Suits The four sections of the Minor Arcana. Each suit represents different qualities and is related to one of the four elements.

Swords A suit of the Minor Arcana associated with the element of air, and related to matters of the mind and intellect.

Synchronicity The theory posited by Carl Jung that everything in the world is connected.

Tarocco The card game from which, it is thought, the Tarot deck developed. The 78-card pack was used in this Italian game.

Tarot de Marseilles A classic Tarot deck dating from the 16th century. It was hugely influential on card designs.

Torah Jewish holy book.

Tree of Life From cabbalist ideology. This visual diagram is a symbolic way of understanding the relationship between the ten sephiroth.

Trump cards The cards of the Major Arcana numbered 1–21, plus the unnumbered Fool card.

Wands A suit of the Minor Arcana associated with the element of Fire, and related to energy, enthusiasm, and action.

Yin and Yang The Chinese principle of masculine and feminine.

FURTHER READING

ALMOND, JOCELYN, & SEDDON, KEITH. *Tarot for Relationships*, The Aquarian Press, 1990

CALVINO, ITALO. *The Castle of Crossed Destinies*, Harcourt, Brace, Jovanovich, 1976

CAVENDISH, RICHARD. *The Tarot*, Michael Joseph, 1975

CROWLEY, ALEISTER. *The Book of Thoth*, U.S. Games Systems, 1977

DECKER, RONALD, DEPAULIS, THIERRY, & DUMMETT, MICHAEL. *A Wicked Pack of Cards*, St Martins, 1996

DOUGLAS, ALFRED. *The Tarot: The Origins, Meaning and Uses*, Penguin, 1972

DUMMETT, MICHAEL. *The Game of Tarot*, U.S. Games Systems, 1980

FAIRFIELD, GAIL. *Choice-Centred Tarot*, Newcastle, 1985

GRAY, EDEN. *Complete Guide to the Tarot*, Bantam, 1971

GREER, MARY K. *Tarot for Yourself*, Newcastle, 1984

HUDSON, PAUL. *The Devil's Picturebook*, G.P. Putnam & Sons, 1971

HUDSON, PAUL. *The Devil's Picturebook*, Sphere, 1972

KNIGHT, GARETH. *The Magical World of Tarot*, The Aquarian Press, 1992

MATHERS, S.L., *Tarot*, Gordon, 1973

MOAKLEY, GERTRUDE. *The Tarot Cards Painted by Bonifacio Bembo*, New York Public Library, 1966

NICHOLS, SALLIE. *Jung and Tarot*, Samuel Weiser, 1981

NOBLE, VICKI. *Motherpeace: A Way to the Goddess Through Myth, Art and Tarot*, Harper and Row, 1983

NORMAN, MARSHA. *The Fortune Teller*, Random House, 1987

O'NEILL, ROBERT V. *Tarot Symbolism*, Fairways Press, 1986

PEACH, EMILY. *The Tarot Workbook*, The Aquarian Press, 1984

POLLACK, RACHEL. *Seventy Eight Degrees of Wisdom* The Aquarian Press, 1980

POLLACK, RACHEL. *Tarot Readings and Meditations*, The Aquarian Press, 1990

POLLACK, RACHEL, & MATTHEWS, CAITLIN. *Tarot Tales*, Random Century, 1989

REED, ELLEN CANNON. *The Witches Tarot*, Llewellyn Publications, 1989

RILEY, JANA. *Tarot Dictionary and Compendium*, Samuel Weiser, 1995

SHARMAN-BURKE, JULIET, & GREENE, LIZ. *The Mythic Tarot Workbook*, Rider, 1986

SHARMAN-BURKE, JULIET. *The Mythic Tarot Workbook*, Rider, 1989.

SHARMAN-BURKE, JULIET. *The Complete Book of Tarot*, Pan Books, 1985

WAITE, A.E. *The Pictorial Key to the Tarot*, Samuel Weiser, 1983

WILLIAMS, CHARLES. *The Greater Trumps*, Gollancz, 1932

WANG, ROBERT. *An Introduction to the Golden Dawn Tarot*, The Aquarian Press, 1978

WANG, ROBERT. *Qabalistic Tarot*, Samuel Weiser 1983

ZIEGLER, GERD. *Tarot: The Mirror of the Soul*, Samuel Weiser, 1988

USEFUL ADDRESSES

Centre for Psychological Astrology
BCM Box 1815 London
WC1 N3XX
(Tel/Fax 00 44 (0)208 749 2330)
www.astrologer.com.cpa
The CPA runs Tarot seminars.

The American Tarot Association
http://www.ata-tarot.com/
A forum for students, teachers, and masters of Tarot.

The Australian Tarot Guild
PO Box 369, East Kew, Victoria, 3102
http://www.alternatives.com.au/Tguild.htm
A network for sharing information on the Tarot.

The Canadian Tarot Network
http://www.tarotcanada.com/
Brings together those interested in Tarot, willing to adhere to high ethical standards.

The International Tarot Society
http://www.geocities.com/Athens/Ithaca/3772/
Aims to improve the practice of Tarot, and also sponsors courses on Tarot.

Introduction to the Tarot
denvid@poetic.com
Send an e-mail for information and advice.

Jungian Tarot Course
entrance@icon.co.za
Send an e-mail for information and advice.

Learning the Tarot
http://www.kasamba.com/
A site dedicated to information on the Tarot with everything that the beginner needs to know.

Learning the Tarot On-line
http://www2.dgsys.com/~bunning/top.html
A course covered in 19 lessons.

Tarot Classes
http://www.tarotschool.com
Offers lessons online, or through correspondence courses.

Tarot Directory
http://tarotfool.com
A forum for advice on getting started.

Tarot Discussions
http://www.facade.com/attraction/tarot
Discussions including how Tarot originated.

Tarot and Healing

http://www.angelpaths.com
A site exploring how the Tarot can be used for the purposes of Healing.

Tarot and Kabbalah

http://members.ficom.net/ditch/tarot.htm
Examines the link between Tarot and the Hebrew Cabbalah.

Tarot Mailing List

http://www.lightspeed.bc.ca/hilander/tarotl.html
A mailing list for discussions about all aspects of Tarot. Subscribers are encouraged to take part in the discussions.

Tarot and Palmistry Readings

http://www.jfinternational.com/psy/homepage_psychic.htm
Readings using Tarot, palmistry, and astrology.

Tarot News and Reviews

http://www.nccn.net/~tarot/
News, reviews, and other resources.

Tarot Readings Online

http://www.tarothaven.com/
A site dedicated to providing the best Tarot readings.

Tarot Reviews

www.nccn.net/~tarot/reviews.html
Holds Tarot clinics, publishes articles, and shows Tarot spreads.

The Tarot Society of South Africa

http://www.tarot.co.za/
Information on Tarot, Healing, and Divination.

Tarot Superstore

http:/search.freefind.com/
Has secure online ordering facilities.

Witches' Web Shop

http:/www.witchesweb.com/
A retail outlet with lots of Tarot paraphernalia on offer.

The World of Tarot and I Ching

http://lightage.com/world_of_tarot/
Also gives information on Runes.

INDEX

ACKNOWLEDGEMENTS

The author would like to thank everyone who has contributed to her learning
of the Tarot. Special thanks to Jane Struthers and Tricia Allen for their invaluable
and much appreciated support.

PICTURE ACKNOWLEDGEMENTS

Every effort has been made to trace copyright holders and obtain permission.
The publishers apologize for any omissions and would be pleased to make any
necessary changes at subsequent printings.

Illustrations from the decks named on the following pages are reproduced by
permission of U.S. Games Systems Inc. Stamford, CT 06902. Further reproduction prohibited.
2, 14/15, 18/19, 22/23, 26/27, 36, 38, 50/51, 54/55, 58/59, 62/63, 66/67,
70/71, 74/75, 78/79, 86/87, 94/95, 98/99, 106, 110, 118/119, 122/123,
134/135, 154, 155, 159, 163, 167, 170/171, 179, 183, 191, 195, 198/199,
206/207, 210/211, 214/215.

Astrological Tarot © 1983, Barbara Walker Tarot ©1986, Egipcios Kier Tarot ©1984,
Golden Dawn Tarot ©1982, Haindl Tarot ©1991, Herbal Tarot 1990, JJ Swiss Tarot © 1974,
Tarot of Marseilles © 1996, Morgan-Greer Tarot © 1993, Motherpeace Tarot © 1996,
Oswald Wirth Tarot © 1976, Papus Tarot © 1983, Tarot of the Spirit © 1996,
Tarot of the Witches © 1994, Ukiyoe Tarot © 1983, Universal Waite © 1990,
Visconti Sforza Tarot © 1975.

Illustrations reproduced by
permission of AGM AGMuller,
CH-8212 Neuhausen, Switzerland.
Further reproduction prohibited ©
AGM, Switzerland/OTO USA.

Aleister Crowley Thoth Tarot: 27R,
39L, 63B, 79M, 90/91,
102/103, 115, 126, 130.

Gipsy Tarot (Zigeuner) 27T, 46R.

Shining Woman:
Rachel Pollack/HarperCollins
Publishers Ltd., 39R.

Picture Credits

AKG, London: 20,39L,174.

**The Bridgeman Art Library,
London:** 43TR (National
Archaeological Museum, Athens),
p.67 Museo Boltracin
& Museo Civico, Padua, 202
William Laurence.

Stone/GettyOne, London:
47B,178.

The StockMarket, London:
55TL:72.